YOUR PATHWAY
— TO —
GROWTH

JACK B MCVICAR

Copyright © 2019 Jack B McVicar

First published in 2019 by Freedom Centre Publishing

The right of Jack McVicar to be identified as the author of this work has been asserted by him in accordance with the Copyright, Designs, and Patents Act 1988.

All rights reserved. No part of this publication may be reproduced, stored in a retrieval system, or transmitted in any other form or by any means, electronic, mechanical, photocopying, recording or otherwise, without the prior permission of the publisher.

British Library Cataloguing in Publication Data
A catalogue record for this book is available from the British Library.

ISBN 978-0-9568025-2-1

Scripture quotation taken from various Bible translations.

Photographs taken at various places including:
Crieff-Scotland, Arta-Majorca, Preston-England.
Additional photos supplied by Ruah Ministries, Chennai.
(www.ruahministries.org)

Stock photography from Pexels (www.pexels.com)

Design and layout by Jonathan Marfleet

Printed by Swallowtail Print Ltd

WHAT OTHERS ARE SAYING

"A vital reminder that no one who claims to follow Jesus can stand still – while we cannot earn grace, we must all learn growth."

J John,
Evangelist

"Jack and Sue truly are kingdom ambassadors. Their heart of love for God and people is contiguous. They spread their passion & compassion in serving God and His people wherever they go. The book *Your Pathway to Growth* is a guide which will challenge anyone who desires to move from mediocrity to excellence, apathy to expectancy. God desires growth and the enemy wants you to remain stagnant. The biblical, yet practical principles Jack gives you in this book will set you free and set you ablaze for God's purposes and glory."

Joseph Naveen,
The Altar-Freedom Life Centre, Chennai

"Good, sound, practical principles on lifestyle, attitude and leadership. Anyone who is aspiring to a greater leadership role will only benefit from reading this book."

Lyndon Bowring,
Care, Executive Chairman

"*Your Pathway to Growth* - is a life guide for growth by a man of God with a great vision to educate, empower, enrich and guide people. After the Bible, there is no other book that has helped grow and guide me like this one. It takes more than just a man who can write with a pen to write a book such as this. It takes someone with real life experience, a servant heart, a shepherd mindset and love for people to produce such a work. I love it!"

Adman. Blessing A Manikandan,
CEO, Paulsons Lifestyle Group (Master Franchisee of TONI&GUY, India)

....

"Compelling, motivating, and reflective - *Your Pathway to Growth* is a must-read for Christians today. Jack McVicar skillfully composes a rich mosaic of principles of growth, putting together piece by piece the path that you need to take to become all that you are destined to be. His practical approach - gleaning invaluable wisdom from the Word of God and his experiences in life and ministry - makes this book authentic and inspiring. If you are looking for a resource to bring about growth and change - as an individual or in the Church - I can say with certainty that this is the book for you! Now is the time to grow."

Pastor Theodore Nathaniel,
ONE Church, Dubai

....

"The teaching of Jack B McVicar has been such a blessing to all of us at Elim Glorious Revival Church in Chennai. I am sure as you read this book you will be challenged and given the opportunity to grow both in your ministry and in your life. I commend it to you."

Pastor Joseph Osborne Jebadurai,
Chennai

"This book is a balanced combination of solid biblical principles and fascinating experiences. It grips you, instructs you, and excites you about what God wants you to do. It makes GROWTH an adventure that leads to maturity and service. As you read this book, you will learn more about the importance of GROWTH in the process of becoming what God wants you to be."

Apostle Jonathan Suppaya,
Apostolic Overseer, Jesus Lives Church, Singapore

"An excellent read. A systematic analysis and a methodical evaluation of life in terms of growth and progress. This book encourages and instils a desire to grow in all spheres of life with biblical values that are applicable for everyone. Without being religious, yet God is the centre of growth and success."

Pastor Prabhu Ganeshan,
Dubai/Abu Dhabi/Hyderabad

"*Your Pathway to Growth*, written by my friend and great man of God, Rev. Jack McVicar, is powerful, eye-opening and it inspires us to relentlessly pursue the dreams and visons God has given to each one of us, especially the believers of Christ and the servants of God.

Pastor Jack's simplicity of writing will make it easy to understand the contents for any reader. The scriptural references and the appropriate quotes of notable people in it, have added depth to such an important topic. I have no doubt this book is going to encourage the potential of every human being who has a heart after Jesus. This will refresh and restore the dreams they once had as well as restore the purpose imparted in their lives. I am expectant to hear the testimonies of blessings that will come out from reading this book.

We pray that many more books such as this will flow from the hands of this wonderful friend for the glory of God. Be blessed and motivated."

Pastor Prabhu Isaac,
Pittsburgh USA

"I am so proud of Jack McVicar – he is not only my brother and my friend, but is also now the author of two books. There are many books you could read on growth, but not many that are so easy to read and so practical. I absolutely love this book and I know you will too – it will give you everything you need to grow deeper."

Nancy Goudie,
Author, Speaker, Founder of Spiritual Health Weekends,
Co-founder of ngm and Inspire Arts Trust

FOREWORD

My wife Joy and I consider it a great pleasure and privilege to pen a few lines of appreciation for the great work my dearest pastor friend and brother Jack B. McVicar has presented here!

I have known Jack and his wife Sue for approximately ten years and they have spoken at our church many times over the years. They always carry a prophetic word for our season and have been a great blessing to us.

Apart from being a great preacher (and an entrepreneur before that), Jack is a prolific writer with a passion to build leaders who will in turn lead others! His last book, 'Learn to Lead', was a valuable teaching tool and was well received by our church members as well as those who lead in the everyday world!

I encourage you to read this new book and benefit from the wise words it contains. Growth is always paramount and indeed vital for every individual or organization. I trust that you will be highly impacted and blessed by my friend's words as you read his thoughts on growth. May your pathway to growth start from here.

Pastor Alwin Thomas,
Chennai

DEDICATIONS

I dedicate this book to my amazing family.

To Sue who I love dearly and who has been my wife and best friend for over 40 years and my co-pastor and fellow founder of our various charities. I thank God for your heart for Jesus and your love for me. What an amazing journey we are having.

To our children, Natalie, Charlene and Tanya, I thank God for each one of you. You are precious to us. To Jon, Will and Jonnie, our girls have chosen well. To our grandchildren, Ruby, Keyah, Caleb and Austin, we love each one of you very deeply.

To my extended McVicar family, we have a wonderful heritage to share and be proud of.

To my spiritual sons, daughters and family at the freedomcentre, you are simply the best.

To my Saviour, my ever present Lord and teacher, you are the one and true God. It's you who has guided me along my own personal pathway to growth. Your grace is and has been simply amazing.

And finally to those who find themselves hurting, distressed and broken. Freedom and growth is God's purpose and desire for you. The world needs your talents and abilities. You are not forgotten.

SPECIAL THANKS

There are so many people who have played a part in this book. This a true team effort. First of all, thanks again to Sue my wife for her constant support and encouragement. You have been continually creative and inspirational.

Thanks to my whole family who have been involved in this book, especially my son in law Jon Marfleet, who has used his amazing skills in the layout of this book. Moreover, thank you to Sue, Natalie, Charlene and Tanya for all your creative ideas and photography. It's been well worth it.

Thanks to Abigail van Kraay and Sam Lee, your editing and analysis has been amazing. Thanks to Heather Lee and Matt Porter, for your media work and creativity and a huge thanks to Pastor Joseph Naveen and his staff at The Altar in Chennai.

To our Vision Team, and also the Trustees of the freedomcentre, Luv Preston and Lydia House Trust charities who are committed to making the vision we have, come to pass.

I am also indebted to the people who have endorsed the book so graciously and so my thanks goes to Pastor Alwin Thomas, Pastor Joseph Osborne Jebadurai and Pastor Joseph Naveen from Chennai, India. Evangelist J.John, Lyndon Bowring and my amazing sister Nancy Goudie from the U.K. Pastor Theodore Nathaniel from Dubai and Pastor Prabhu Ganeshan who pastors in Dubai, Abu Dhabi and Hyderabad. Pastor Prabhu Isaac from Pittsburgh USA as well as Pastor Jonathan Suppaya from Singapore. I also appreciate the very kind endorsement from my amazing friend and businessman Adman Blessing A Manikandan the CEO of Paulsons Lifestyle Group, the master franchisee of Toni & Guy in India.

Finally to Bishop T.D. Jakes, your influence has been immeasurable, your loyalty, commitment and wise words to Sue and I as our spiritual father, has been life changing over these past 16 years. Thank you so much for all your kindness to us.

CONTENTS

Foreword by *Pastor Alwin Thomas* 6

Dedications 7

Special thanks 9

Introduction 13

Growth by thinking differently 17

Growth by talking differently 31

Growth through your terrors 43

Growth through training and teaching 51

Growth through teamwork 59

Growth through tears 69

Growth through textbooks 79

Growth through being thankful 87

Growth through thoroughness 95

Growth for today 105

Growth beyond your tradition 115

Growth through travel 123

Growth through time 131

Conclusion 141

YOUR PATHWAY TO GROWTH

INTRODUCTION

I am thrilled and deeply thankful that you have chosen to pick up this book. My earnest desire is that, as a result of reading and applying this book, you will see amazing growth in your life.

Growth is not an automatic process; it's for those who desire and decide to grow. The way you decide to read this book will determine what you receive from it. If you read it with slight interest the results you receive will be very small. If you read it with a deep desire to grow as a human being then I know you will see very positive results. Read it as a piece of material that has the potential to change large parts of you. They say a shark will never grow out of its environment. If it is put in a fish tank, then it will grow to 8 inches, but if it is released into the ocean where it really belongs, it will grow to 8 feet. You are no different, please believe that.

It is sad to say that not everyone has the desire to expand. They are unhappy, but they still stay where they are. The desire to grow is there, but they stunt their growth because they somehow feel trapped in their unhappiness; some even wallow and bathe in it, and it's become their 'happy tank'. They say, "it is what it is," "I will never forgive," or "I just can't forget". These statements indicate that they have settled for less rather than the abundance of what God promises and wants to us experience. Some people seem happy to be unhappy. It's the

seduction of what I call 'pseudo safety'. It isn't real, it is in fact depleting, draining and depressing.

This book is written for the one who wants to break out of that 'happy tank' go forward and win. It is written for the one who wants to reap their reward and see their lives enlarge and their circumstances change for good. It's for the one who doesn't ask how long the journey will take, but rather - how far can they travel? It's for the one who doesn't want to be left behind. It's for the one who faces the future and wonders - "do I have what it takes?" It's for the prodigal who is on his way back and is not yet sure of the welcome ahead.

This is for all of us, because we all have great potential that needs revealing and releasing. There can come a time in our lives - and it can come anytime - when we decide that we will no longer just hang around waiting to become the person we dream to be. We can suddenly conclude, that today is the day I will start the journey towards being the person I truly want to be. My friends, my enemies, my family, my church and my mistakes have assisted me on my journey of progression. I don't always enjoy my development and you won't always either; growth can be hard, but it can also be satisfying. If you are prepared to learn and get out of the box that you are currently in - you will increase too.

When you limit yourself by not facing challenges, avoiding mistakes, not educating yourself, not forgiving, not apologising, and not breaking out of that comfortable tank you are in, you stagnate. Don't remain small, stunted or hemmed in - you are meant for growth, as Anaïs Nin beautifully put it,

"And the day came when the risk to remain tight in a bud was more painful than the risk it took to blossom."

It's not easy, but if you are determined, proactive and relentless in your decision to grow then you will flourish. Do not just change your habits, although you will realise as you read this book that many habits must change. You must go much deeper, you must change your mind. If you do, you will be the one reaching the higher level, making things happen and gaining ground. The late Jim Rohn said,

"Success is something you attract rather than something you pursue." You have to decide to change the current you, to be able to grow into the potential you.

INTRODUCTION

As I am writing this introduction; I am travelling to India. I needed more power for my computer, so I asked the flight attendant where I could re-charge the battery. She kindly showed me a power point plug by the screen in front of me. It was right in front of me, but I couldn't see it.

I am praying that this book right in front of you, will be a connection point that will empower you on your future journey of growth. It's time to leave your self-inflicted tank and give yourself permission to grow.

We are going to re-build you, project you forward and see you grow. You are meant to be greater than average and because of this book, I believe you will grow way above average. Average gives you average results. If you can become above average, you will achieve results above average. If you reach greatness you can see great results. Growth doesn't come from reading text but by living it. Robin Sharma puts it this way:

"Ideation without execution is delusion."

In other words, if you have the idea but you do nothing about it, all you are doing is deluding yourself. Don't just read each chapter; make it part of your life; integrate it into your daily experience and you will grow! You are more than the sum of your current circumstances. So, let's make a start today on YOU becoming all that you can be by growing into your destiny.

CHAPTER ONE

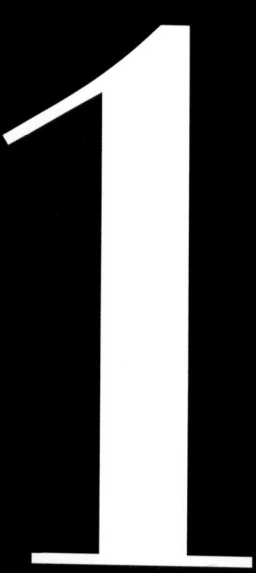

GROWTH BY THINKING DIFFERENTLY

YOUR DREAM LIFE STARTS HERE

YOUR PATHWAY TO **GROWTH**

GROWTH BY THINKING DIFFERENTLY

Hugh walked into the room and after not seeing him for many years I began to realise he hadn't grown. Yes, he had grown physically; he had even grown a family, but I could tell very quickly his thinking hadn't grown at all. The insecurity was there, the rejection, the inferiority complex and the depressing demeanour. He had a chip on his shoulder which you couldn't see, and he was suffering some medical complaints which you could see.

As I began to talk to Hugh and give him some positive thoughts, he would quickly seek to shoot them down with his ingrained negativity. He talked a lot, but it was flavoured with pessimism. My heart went out to him, but as I tried to speak positively into his situation, I realised his mind was caged in. He really wasn't listening to me at all and when he was silent, he was waiting for me to finish talking, so he could continue with his own thoughts of despair. As I watched him limping away, I realised he was just as much limping inwardly as he was outwardly.

I then found my mind going to Nelson Mandela who was incarcerated for twenty-six years, mostly on Robben Island in solitary confinement. One of his wardens said to him when he arrived, "This is the island, this is where you will die!" What would destroy and kill others, didn't kill Nelson Mandela. He didn't die - you could argue he learned how to live. He re-entered back into society after all those years, not negatively but positively. He once said, "I went for a long holiday!" He had gained so much wisdom from twenty-six years of reflection. What you gain inwardly is immeasurable when you decide to learn positively from the misery and pain that often can come to a human life. Once when he was taken to see his lawyer who was visiting him, he was escorted by eight wardens. Two were in front of him, two on either side and two at the back. As he entered his lawyer's presence he said, "You know, George, this place really has made me forget my manners. I haven't introduced you to my guard of honour." It's what happens in you and not what happens to you that is important. Painful times can be the most life changing if you think right.

Have you ever tired of thinking the same old thoughts every day? Majoring in minors? Seeing the negatives rather than the positives? As you analyse your thought life, I wonder if you are content or unhappy with the thoughts that go through your mind each day? Are you thinking the same thoughts you were thinking five years ago? Are you progressing in your thinking? Is your thought life contributing positively or negatively to your personal life, family life, business life or your studies? It's been said that negative thoughts such as jealousy, fear, worry and anxiety destroy nerves and glands, and bring about different mental and physical diseases. ('Expand the power of your subconscious mind.' by C. James Jenson)

Our thought life has not happened by accident. It's the result of many years of the same old undisciplined thinking. Our thoughts are often like stones and boulders that come to the surface of our mind from the burial of events, situations, relationships or declarations of the past. How people have treated you, how you were discouraged or encouraged. The learning you sat under. What you have read, watched, listened to. The way life has treated you and your reaction to it. Your thoughts have taken – and are taking – you on a journey. The question is: Do you like the destination you are heading to, or even where it has brought you thus far? Your thought life is the GPS system which drives you to your destination, whether you really intend to go there or not.

James Allen put it this way:
"You are today where your thoughts have brought you; you will be tomorrow where your thoughts take you!"

You will always grow to the level and the quality of your thinking. Success and failure begin first in your mind. It's as if your conscious mind is the security guard to your subconscious mind. Your conscious mind allows your subconscious mind the information it thinks is acceptable. If you are allowing all sorts of invasive and negative thoughts legitimacy and presenting then to your subconscious as fact, then prepare yourself for the fallout. Small thoughts lead to small actions. Great thoughts lead to great actions.

YOUR PATHWAY TO GROWTH

So, if you personally want to grow, and I assume you do as you are reading this book, then first you must address how you are thinking. The Bible says, "As a man thinks in his heart, so is he!"

That means, quite simply, you can change as a person through thinking differently. If you are keen to grow, and I assume you are, then your development needs, first and foremost, to change in your thought life. When you begin to control your thoughts, you start to control your mind. When you do that, you then realise that you are controlling your life.

Your mind is your hard drive – as in your computer – so the thoughts you put in there are crucial. If you put rubbish in, rubbish, I am afraid, does come out! Your 'hard drive' mind can be corrupted, it can get viruses, it can become clogged up. Your mind is precious and needs to be protected. You need security software for your mind. What you read, what you watch, who befriends you, what relationships you have and conversations you get involved in. All these situations have possibilities for good and bad for your mindset.

Even the conversations you have with yourself. You do realise everyone speaks to themselves; the trick is not to do it out loud. If you do that, people will be worried! Everyone speaks to themselves, but what everyone doesn't always realise is: your communication is creating your future. We all should know what you confess publicly is important, but what we often don't realise is our non-verbal communication to ourselves is vital too. If you keep telling yourself that you cannot pass the exam, get the promotion, buy the house or get the partner, then your subconscious takes that as a fact and these events become harder to bring to reality. There is a reason Jesus said, "As your faith so be it!"

Where you are today is where your thoughts have brought you, and it will be the same tomorrow and the rest of your days until your thoughts and inner conversation changes.

Can I encourage you to stop the negative thoughts? "How?" I hear you say! "I have always been this way." You always will be, unless you decide, and that decision can be made even by you. It needs a decision to be made. That decision needs to be communicated internally and externally. You need – not just every day, but every hour of the day – to be communicating what and who you desire to have the mindset to be.

GROWTH BY THINKING DIFFERENTLY

Successful athletes, business people, professionals, anyone who has risen to the top of their field, decided, then followed through on that decision. If the road was rough, so be it. If times got hard then that was OK. If people created obstacles, they told themselves, "I will overcome these objections, criticisms, unbelief and jealousy." They spoke inwardly far more than they spoke outwardly, about their commitment to the decision they had made. If, at the beginning, the mind interrupted or doubted or was negative in any way, they simply continued to speak more positively to themselves and overcame their previous negative thought life in due course.

Start to form your positive thoughts and your positive thoughts will, through time, form you! Be systematic in your thinking life. Be logical, be consistent, be disciplined. Don't be thoughtless. Be literally thought-full. Fill your mind with Kingdom thoughts and truths. Bury God's word deep into your mind. Sow it for future revelation and harvest. Growth takes time, so that's why it's important that you start immediately. I was brought up to read God's word diligently, but I was never told why it was so important. What the benefits were. How my mind, my attitude and my development would compound positively, every day I disciplined myself to fill my mind with the great truths the Bible contains.

Decisions like reading quality truths decide your future. Growth doesn't just happen, it takes time and perseverance. People so often want immediate blessings and growth. They want instant benefits to manifest in their lives. It really doesn't work that way. Growth comes through systematically thinking right thoughts and then acting on them. Decide to grow your thinking so that success will come to you in time. The world seeks success, but if you change your thinking, I believe success will come to you. God has a plan for your life. People often ask me how they can discover the plan for their life. There is simply no need. God has your plan. What you need to do is discover Him. He tells us His plan is to prosper us, give us hope and give us a future. That seems a pretty good plan to me, so why seek another plan, when God already has one? It's far better to seek God Himself and He says when you do that, all the other things that concern you will come to you! You don't need to stress, you just need to change your thinking and you will grow spiritually, emotionally, financially and physically. The Bible says, "Our beloved, I pray for you that you will prosper in all things and be well, just as your soul prospers." Your soul is your desires, your emotions, your thinking; grow and mature your thinking and God will grow and mature you in every other way.

When you see, feel or perceive something new, your conscious mind refers what

YOUR PATHWAY TO GROWTH

you see or feel to your subconscious mind for analysis. Should I be fearful? Should I accept? Should I resist? And so forth. Once we have that feedback, we decide on either action, inaction or reaction.

It's like asking a search engine. I ask Google all sorts of questions during the day. Well, you also do that with your subconscious too. You may be confronted with a problem or issue and your conscious mind goes to your subconscious mind and begins to ask questions. If your subconscious mind is filled with God's word and God's wisdom, you will find yourself getting the right answers. If your subconscious hasn't had that good investment, then guess what answers you will get? You will get negativity, fear, depression, mistrust and so forth. So, if you have told your subconscious constantly:

- I never will have a good job
- I am always ill
- I have no creativity
- I will never achieve my goals
- I will never have good friends
- I am fat
- I am weak
- I never want more money because money is greed
- I am a failure
- I haven't got a chance
- It won't work out
- I will never find love
- I am too old
- I am too young

and any other version of negativity you have created and believed, then when you go to withdraw from your mind next time you need self-encouragement, guess what will come at you? All that you have invested in your thinking, you will start to withdraw.

Remember: rubbish in, rubbish out.
However, if you decide to take God's thoughts on board and deliver that to your mind to store, then eternal and supernatural thinking are at your disposal.

Supernatural realities like:

- I am well
- I am healed
- I am rich
- I am creative
- I am a new creation
- I am the head and not the tail
- I am successful
- I have a purpose
- I am prosperous
- I have a hope
- I have a future
- I am righteous
- I can do all things
- I am loved
- I am just the right age
- I will win
- I will succeed

Then, when you go to the bank of your mind, all those positive investments will come back to you – and with interest too. You will subsequently find yourself growing.

That's how God operates, Isaiah 14:24 KJV puts it this way: "Surely, as I have thought, so it shall come to pass, and as I have purposed, so it shall stand!"

Remember, God knew you before you were in your mother's womb. That means before your mother and father had any kind of relationship with you, God was intimately involved with you personally. He knew His plans for you. He knew what He wanted you to achieve. He knew why you should be born when and where you were. He knew everything about you - all your potential and possibilities. He thought about you before you were born, before you were planned or unplanned and He thought about you before you had a single thought about Him. Nobody is a mistake. Nobody is a slip up, a blunder or a miscalculation. Not when God is involved in your existence. Before you were a twinkle in your father's eye, you were a thought in your Heavenly Father's mind.

Godly thoughts lead to godly actions, but before the Godly thoughts will come to you,

YOUR PATHWAY TO GROWTH

the thoughts need to be stored in the 'hard drive' of your mind. So many people want to grow, but they don't feed themselves the nutrients to enable their thought life to grow. We need to learn to grow by appreciating that our conscious and subconscious mind is the store that we draw from in order to make progress in our day-to-day life.

Christians often think that an hour on a Sunday morning will feed them for the rest of the week. Sure, one hour on a Sunday is better than nothing, but imagine if you only had one meal a week, how would you cope physically? As it is in the physical, so it is in the spiritual. You need to be 'cooking' your own meals during the week and feeding your mind with good food that will help you grow. Many of us have junk thinking and junk actions because we are eating junk thought food. Learn to grow by changing your thinking; that comes by eating and digesting good thoughts. Do this day after day and you will find yourself having good, positive thoughts that will take you to a higher level.

When this starts to happen, you will find random wrong, impure, negative, ungodly thoughts work their way to your mind. Don't feel condemned, take control.

Every thought must be taken captive. You are now the guardian of your mind. You are checking what goes in and you are also checking what comes out too. When rubbish comes out it is only garbage coming to the surface. Take it captive and replace it with a positive fact. For example, if one day you feel you are unable to cope with your weak financial situation and the thought comes to mind that you are going downhill financially, then replace that thought with "I can do all things through Christ who strengthens me!" That's the context of that verse found in Philippians 4:13. Paul had discovered the way to be content with much and with little. Many financially rich people I have met have been deeply unhappy. Many poor people are dreaming of having more money and being rich. The answer to contentment is not what riches you have; the answer is having the shalom of God in our lives.

Your beliefs work out in the physical. The disciples, when they were struggling to do what Jesus did, said "I believe, help my unbelief!" In the long term, your life is a picture of what you believe. In fact, eternity will reveal to you and to others what you truly believed.

I cannot finish this chapter without speaking about thinking alone. How much thinking do you do productively alone? Many times, we are thinking but not positively. I am talking about having a place that you go to where you have a pad and a pen, and you literally think productively. You need a thinking chair. A definite place where you go over what you are learning. I have a couch in my office where I go to relax, think, pray and contemplate what I have purposefully placed in my mind through what I have heard or read. If you do that in a relaxed place and in a relaxed manor, your thinking will teach you new concepts and thoughts that will add to what you have learned. You will personalise it and make it go deeper in your life.

Write your thoughts down. Even if they are nonsense at first, that doesn't matter because the principle you are learning is more important than what you are writing. In time, the quality of your writing will fall into line with the subject you are thinking through and the quality will improve. Your value to the world is in your perception of what you see, hear and read. People can access others, but they haven't heard your considered thinking.

Personal growth comes by deciding, "I am worth investing in," and if that means sitting down in a nice chair and looking out of the window and thinking productively, so be it. One note to finish on is to make sure that the content of your thinking is good for you. Good reading and good listening precede good thinking. What I mean by that is to make sure you stock up on thinking food that is positive and wholesome. If you just start thinking without storing up something positive to consider, you will just end up mulling over the garbage and the dregs of your life. Remember: rubbish in means rubbish out. You are addicted to your thoughts, so make sure your addiction is working for you.

As your thinking grows, your confidence will increase, and life will begin to offer you opportunities to share your newly developed thoughts. Your thoughts will start to be in demand because people will recognise that you have something to offer that they need. That means because you decided to grow, others grow too. Their thinking and their learning have new possibilities, just because you picked out a place to go to think through personally what you have been learning.

Most people don't think, they just act. They will say things like "I just felt like it!" or "It seemed a good idea at the time!" You will have heard the old saying "Act in haste; repent at leisure!" and the reason you have heard it is because it's true. Thinking is your friend, not your enemy. It will propel you forward, not backwards. It will take you to the next dimension. Decide to become thoughtful as you learn to grow. It's the first step.

Actions to help you GROW in your THINKING

1 Analyse where your past thinking has brought you, good and bad. Write down 5 positive results of thinking positively and likewise write down 5 negative results of thinking negatively.

2 Make the decision to stop negative thinking. Act on this decision by writing it down, declaring your intention to choose positivity over negativity. Then date this declaration and tell someone close to you who can hold you accountable.

3 Make a list of positive thoughts that you need to start to think about at the beginning of each day.

4 Develop your daily thinking programme. When will you think? What time and place? What will you sacrifice to make the time?

5 Choose a thinking chair that you can go to.

"The world as we have created it is a process of our thinking. It cannot be changed without changing our thinking."

- Albert Einstein -

Quotes on Thinking Differently

"Change your thoughts and you change your world."

- Norman Vincent Peale -

"What we dwell on is who we become."

- Oprah Winfrey -

"Five percent of the people think; ten percent of the people think they think; and the other eighty-five percent would rather die than think."

- Thomas A. Edison -

"Most of man's miseries derive from his inability to sit in a quiet room alone."

- Blaise Pascal -

GROWTH BY THINKING DIFFERENTLY

"Simple can be harder than complex. You have to work hard to get your thinking clean to make it simple. But it's worth it in the end because once you get there, you can move mountains."

- Steve Jobs -

························ **CHAPTER TWO** ························

GROWTH BY TALKING DIFFERENTLY

WORDS MATTER!

Live LOVE Laugh
PORSCHE
GER POR
FERDINAND PORSCHE
Freshly Brewed
Cappuccino Espresso Cafe Latte
Classic Italian Coffee
How Great would life be if we lived a little of it Everyday
ENJOY THIS DAY
Be present
BREATHE DEEPLY
Show gratitude
Live with intention
BE FEARLESS
TRY NEW THINGS
LOVE
MY KIDS HAVE PAWS
LIVE LOVE Laugh
COUNT YOUR BLESSINGS
BE kind to one another
EPH. 4:32
WAKE UP SAY A PRAYER AND HUSTLE
LIFE BEGINS AFTER COFFEE
HAPPY WIFE HAPPY LIFE
Never stop MAKING Wishes
DREAMS DON'T WORK UNLESS YOU DO
FIND BLISS IN BLOOMS
KEEP YOUR SUNNY SIDE UP
LIFE BRINGS US TO UNEXPECTED PLACES LOVE BRINGS US HOME
Live them
Family is all the love you need
Friendship
IF YOUR DREAMS DON'T SCARE YOU THEY'RE NOT BIG ENOUGH
All our dreams can come true
Walt Disney

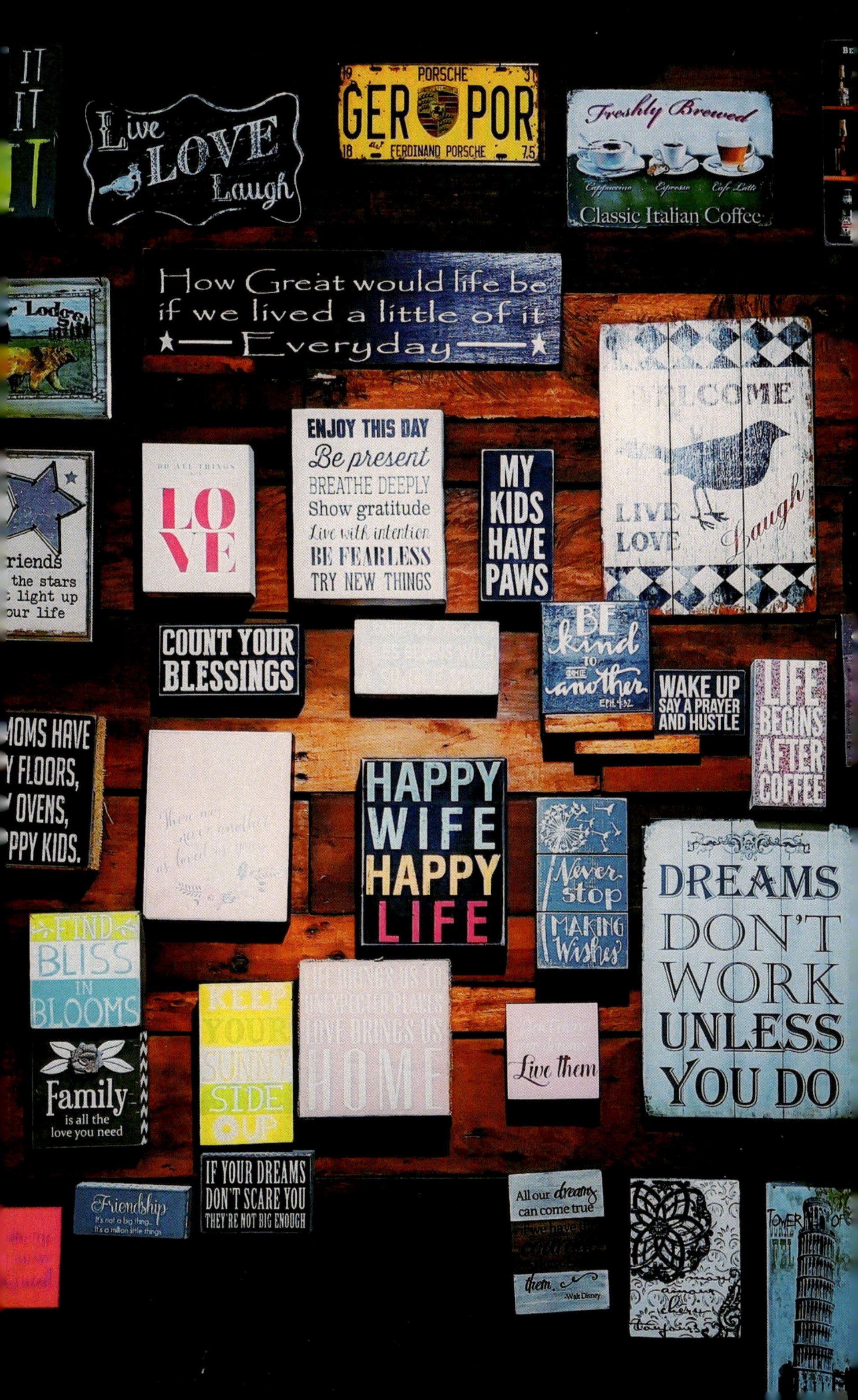

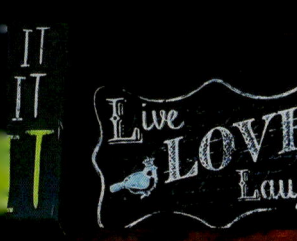

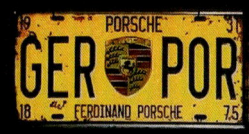

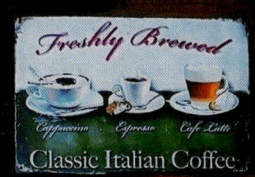

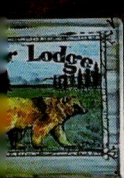

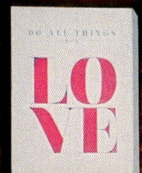

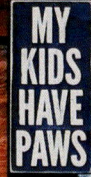

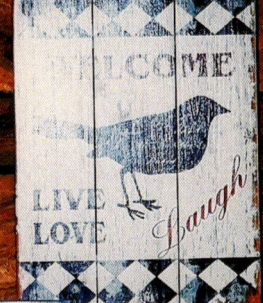

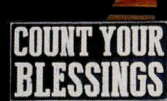

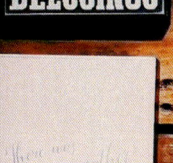

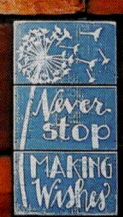

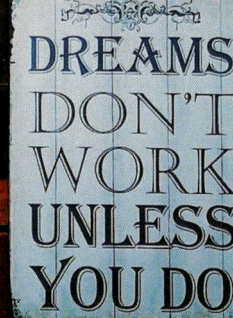

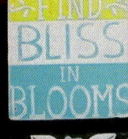

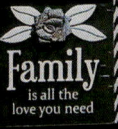

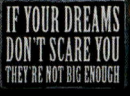

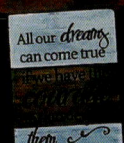

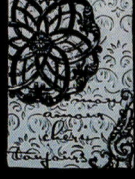

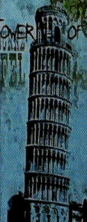

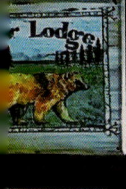

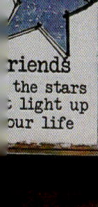

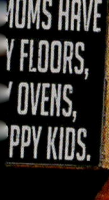

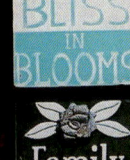

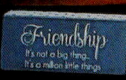

GROWTH BY TALKING DIFFERENTLY

Words matter! They are powerful and can inspire incredible feats and lift people, or they can destroy an individual or a relationship. Isn't it amazing how you make a judgement on someone as soon as they start talking? Your talking has helped create your own personal world. You may be unaware, but you make a determination on someone when they start talking: whether they are strong or weak, rich or poor, educated or uneducated, spiritual or non-spiritual, caring or uncaring, where they are from and where they are going – all from their communication. You decide even whether they like you or dislike you. Words are vital and important. They set the agenda for our lives. They can inspire, depress, motivate and set the tone and the mood in a room or a relationship.

Hearing yourself inwardly is important but hearing yourself outwardly is important too. Speaking outwardly achieves much more than you would instantly appreciate. The Bible constantly talks about confession.

"If you will CONFESS with your mouth the Lord Jesus you shall be saved!" Why does the Bible consider confession so important? Why is our talking and what we confess from our lips so important? It's because:

Confession commits you.
Confession makes you accountable.
Confession sets deadlines.
Confession sets goals.
Confession reveals vision.
Confession reveals friends to go to and enemies to avoid.
Confession brings resources.

Money and resources will always follow vision and what you confess. Money and resources will disappear when there is division, denial and silence.

Some people, however, talk big but never achieve anything like what they confess because they never really believed it themselves. The saying is: "they are full of hot air". In fact, they talk big but never think big. They bypass any thought process.

Unless you committed and activated chapter 1, there is no point in reading this chapter. Unless we have internalised it, there is no growth in externalising it. There are many reasons to commit to talking and confessing, and the above are just a few of them.

At this moment I am writing this chapter in India. I have been talking about 'growth' and teaching people the above principles. I have, for several years, been thinking about writing this book, so I have put into practice what I am teaching you. I have been publicly confessing that next time I visit India I will have written and published the book I have been thinking about. That confession has committed me. It has made me accountable to many hundreds of people. It has given me a deadline. It has set me a vision and a goal. It has given me the appetite to write where before there was none. I was always thinking of writing my second book, but until I spoke my thoughts and 'talked my thoughts', the appetite just wasn't there.

The book will also reveal new friends and perhaps new enemies too. I also believe the resources needed to enable me to publish this book will reveal themselves at the appropriate time. In fact, since I wrote this last sentence someone has offered to design the cover and print the book. The very fact that you are reading this book and – I hope – benefiting from it is because I have put into practice the very principles I am teaching you.

Have a listen to what you are confessing in your daily life. Does what you confess add or subtract to what you believe? Out of the heart the mouth speaks. If you are storing up great thinking and then you are marrying that thinking to your speaking, you are into multiplication.

I love the statement from American author Susie Larson. She states:

"I am deeply loved, divinely appointed, abundantly equipped, and profoundly cherished by God. No enemy plan, scheme, or obstacle can keep me from God's highest and best will for me. As I follow the voice of my Saviour, I see the invisible, accomplish the impossible, and love the unlovable. I am a living-breathing miracle because Jesus Christ lives in me!"

If you would believe and confess that statement every morning and evening into the bathroom mirror, you would see a different person looking back at you.

As Christians, we may believe and think that statement is theologically true, but we never speak it over ourselves. In our best moments we tell someone else but rarely speak it to ourselves.

Build on great thinking with great talking and what happens is you literally talk yourself upwards. The opposite also true. If you marry negative talking with negative thinking, then you are going down to the basement level.

- I can't do it.
- I can never do it.
- I won't pass.
- I can't lose weight.
- I am rubbish.
- I won't get promotion.
- I'll never have any money.
- I hate myself.

These are untrue, idle words. The Bible says we must account for every idle word. If you read Matthew 12, you will see several important points. We learned earlier that out of the abundance of the heart the mouth speaks. We see if you have stored good treasure, you speak out good things. We also see the opposite is true as well. Then Jesus says we will give account and by our words we will be justified (or see growth) and by our words we will be condemned (see no growth).

Psalm 50 v 23
"Whoso offereth praise glorifieth me; and to him that ordereth his conversation aright, I will show the salvation of God." KJV

Proverbs 18 v 20-21
"A man's stomach shall be satisfied from the fruit of his mouth; from the produce of his lips he shall be filled. Death and life are in the power of the tongue, and those who love it will eat its fruit." NKJV

Your words make a pathway for you to travel down. Speak God's truth and you are on the side of the only opinion that counts. When we speak His truth, we are partnering with Him. The negative, diminishing, self-critical words you sometimes say over yourself have the opposite effect. Have you ever noticed that if you are negative, people shy away from you eventually; they literally shrink away from your presence? They see you coming, and they think, "How can I avoid this person? Their words cause negativity, their words cause depression, their words bring death instead of life." Yet when you decide to be positive and constantly sow good positive statements into people, they will seek you out to be encouraged. People need encouragement and they will pay you in different ways for what they need. The fact is you need to encourage because it's through that positive talking that you and your life will grow.

Let me give you an example of how words can get a positive reaction:

YOUR PATHWAY TO **GROWTH**

I came across these two stories recently.

1 A man on vacation was strolling along outside his hotel. Suddenly, he was attracted by the screams of a woman kneeling in front of a child. The man knew enough to determine that the child had swallowed a coin. Seizing the child by the heels, the man held him up, gave him a few shakes, and a quarter dropped to the sidewalk. "Oh, thank you sir!" cried the woman. "You seemed to know just how to get it out of him. Are you a doctor?" No, ma'am," replied the man, "I'm with the Tax Authorities."

2 Two men were marooned on an island. One man paced back and forth like he thought it was the last day of his life, while the other man relaxed and appeared unconcerned. The first man said to the second man, "Aren't you afraid? We are about to die." "No," said the second man, "I made a £100,000 commitment to our church building fund. My pastor will definitely find me."

Did you find yourself smiling when you read these words? maybe you even laughed! If you are a preacher or a teacher, maybe you even thought, "I could use that story." Words produce a reaction, positively or negatively.

If I had told you a sad story of someone's death or illness or crisis, your reaction would have been different. You would have been sad, maybe even slightly depressed. Do you see the power of words? Use negative words carefully and positive words liberally.

I met someone the other day and I told him truthfully, he was looking well. The

GROWTH BY TALKING DIFFERENTLY

first time he laughed. A few minutes later I said it again and he said, "You think so?" I said, "Yes, I do." He still wasn't smiling. Ten minutes later I said it again after he had told me how God had healed his body many years ago. This time there was a physical reaction. He sat up in his seat and smiled. An hour or so later we were in the company of someone else and again I said how well he was looking, and he said, "Yes, I feel well!"

Learn to chat positively. There is so much negative chatter you hear. Ignore it. In fact, when you hear negative talk, decide there and then to say something positive to negate the depressing talk aired by others. Speak positive truth. It changes the verbal atmosphere. Avoid criticism by and of others. It's a waste of your time and talk. There is something that happens physically to people who are constantly negative. Their bodies react to their speech. I believe it's a physical manifestation of an inner reality. If you are constantly hearing negatives, your body physically reacts to that constant verbal sewage. Why would any of us want to feed ourselves sewage? Negative criticism is not a gift, it's a curse. Yes, sometimes we must advise, counsel and even admonish, but constantly offering negativity is not part of God's remit for your life. You harm yourself and those around you when you go down that road. It's not a pathway for the person who wants to grow. It's stunting your future growth and you will never become better than the criticism that you are giving. It's a barrier to you. It puts up obstacles to your future success. Learn to talk differently and learn to talk positively.

Learn to encourage yourself every day. Give yourself rewards for right behaviour, thinking and, indeed, talking. I read somewhere that by the time you reached seventeen years of age you had heard the phrase "no, you can't" an average of 150,000 times. That's a lot of negativity with regards to your ability. What was even more depressing was the news that you only heard "yes, you can" about 5,000 times. So, for every 'yes' you heard 30 'noes'! That's one of the reasons – a very powerful reason – you often feel you can't. That needs to change and what you need to hear from me, from friends, from partners, from books and from yourself is, "YES YOU CAN!"

Your future self will also pay homage to a new discipline and wisdom of learning when to speak up and when to remain silent. Practice increasing your encouragement and reducing your criticism every day. Declare truth, yes, but do it with kindness and the understanding you would want to receive if someone was advising you. Often, people don't hear what we say because they cannot get

YOUR PATHWAY TO GROWTH

beyond the spirit in which the advice is being given.

Some people seem to be putting the whole world to rights. They spend their whole lives proffering their so-called wisdom. I find myself doing this in the car as I drive along, and my wife, Sue, tells me off. Sometimes wisdom begins when we shut our mouths and begin to silently pray for the person who we want to give the benefit of our advice. The exact same goes for self-criticism too. Many of us don't battle so much with criticising others; it's ourselves that we are constantly ripping apart. It begins first thing in the morning and it lasts until night-time. Second guessing our actions, thinking through and analysing every little action. We talk to ourselves and we are telling ourselves: you aren't good enough, you aren't talented enough, you will never keep it up, you will never get the job done, others are bigger and better than you. All this talk is literally defeating your future before God can unveil it to you. If God has placed you where you are, made you who you are, knows why you are you, then shut up and don't tear down what God is building with your words of self-doubt and criticism. What is man (including your inner man) that you are mindful of him? Stop giving yourself excuses to fail. Stop being a coward. Life is not about you: if you are a Christian, it's about Him. I would rather fail doing something that He has called and placed me in than succeed at something I called myself to and had decided that was all I was capable of.

Every disciple of Jesus in the New Testament tried to talk themselves out of their future. It's been tried far too many times, so don't you try it. Every day, your talk sets the agenda and the weather over you for the day. Start the day with negative talk and you immediately start to rain on someone else's parade. You set an agenda for the day that is difficult to adjust. If your words are toxic, they create a toxic environment. So, don't be careless with your words: train yourself to be careful.

Watch how amazing leaders like Nelson Mandela, Mother Teresa and Martin Luther King with their careful talking changed environments and even nations. Compare that with the words of Hitler, Idi Amin and Pol Pot. All were leaders, but one group initiated good and positivity and the other evil and negativity with their mouths.

GROWTH BY TALKING DIFFERENTLY

- Jesus was ruthless when the disciples tried to go against His positive agenda.
- When they wanted to call down fire from heaven, He rebuked them.
- When they wanted to send the children away, He called the children to Him.
- When the Pharisees wanted Him to condemn the woman who was caught in adultery, He admonished the men who hadn't yet been caught.

Can you see the difference between people who haven't got control of their mouths and the words Jesus spoke? Jesus knew that the talk that came out of His mouth had power to heal and restore, but it also had power to hurt, condemn and undermine a person's future. You are no different, so grow your talk. Try it and see the difference in your relationships with those around you. It won't be easy at first. A bad habit takes time to change. A good habit and routine take time to grow. Decide to invest the time to take the higher and, yes, harder road. The higher the road, the better the view at the top. You can literally talk yourself out of the valley your negative words have taken you to. Positive and life-giving talk will position you to go to a higher place. Release the dream-stealing talk and let it go, and capture and then give away to yourself and to others the richness of purity and praise that can grow you. Speak life not death. You cannot build a great building if you are in the business of demolition. God wants you to be a builder and a restorer, not a demolisher of people's lives and dreams. If you use your talk to bring others down and demolish the little project they are trying to build, then you will become a demolition expert. That is not your calling. Your calling is to build up and restore broken hearts and lives. Your talk will play a major part in that construction. Positive and constructive talk are the bricks to build the tallest building you can possibly build. If you will do that for others, then you will find your own building reaching the sky too.

Negative talking people live in the ghettos of dismay and destruction. Positive talking people look up, build up and reach up to take themselves and others to a higher level. There is a reason the penthouse is on the top floor and the basement is at the bottom. The view is much better up there.

If you decide to demolish and crush others, they will never help you build. In fact, often they will make it their personal mission to destroy what you are trying to build. Let your destructive words be few and your constructive words many. The Bible informs us that we will have to give an account of every idle and negative word. Growth comes in your life when you decide to monitor your speech.

Let God use your words to change the atmosphere, grow others and, at the same time, grow you. It's a win-win situation.

YOUR PATHWAY TO GROWTH

Actions to help you GROW in your TALKING

1 Write down three idle words or statements you are prone to say and decide to eliminate them from your daily speech, then tear the paper up and throw it away.

2 Start to speak out daily what God has said about you.

3 On one side of a sheet of paper, write the negative statements you are prone to say, and on the other side write the positive statements you need to start making. When you do this, you will see what you say to yourself, written in black and white.

4 Publicly declare one aim or goal you have that will help you grow.

5 Decide you will talk positively or keep quiet.

> Quotes on your Talking

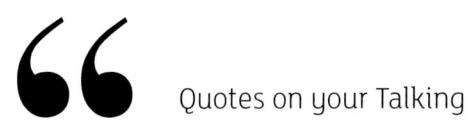

"Think before you speak!

From the same mouth come blessings and cursing. My brothers these things ought not to be so."

- James 3 v 10 -

"If I speak what is false, I must answer for it; if truth, it will answer for me."

- Thomas Fuller -

"Words that do not give the light of Christ increase the darkness."

- Mother Teresa -

"Your self-talk is the channel of behaviour change."

- Gino Norris -

CHAPTER THREE

3

GROWTH THROUGH YOUR TERRORS

TERROR IS YOUR ENEMY

> "Better hazard once than always be in fear."
>
> - Thomas Fuller -

YOUR PATHWAY TO GROWTH

GROWTH THROUGH YOUR TERRORS

For years I was apprehensive about doing certain things - speaking in public was one of them. I didn't know that public speaking was the number one fear for most people. The public speakers I knew, didn't tell me they were terrified at first, and none of them saw any potential in me to speak publicly.

16 years ago, I would have laughed if you had said I would travel the world with my wife, speaking to thousands and writing books. These days I find it just as easy to speak to ten thousand people, as I do ten. I never imagined that I could grow bold enough and good enough to be invited to communicate at all to any audience.

However, I learned to grow into it and now it fits me. It neither impresses me or fills me with terror. In the early days I was petrified. I was more aware of myself than the content of what I was trying to communicate; I was embarrassed, nervous and petrified, but I now see that this was inverted pride. I didn't want to fail. I wanted to impress the audience. I was too consumed with thinking about what they thought.

These days I am more anxious about what God thinks. I am far more concerned about communicating what is on God's heart than my own. In the past I wanted to go straight into being the best, without going through the important failures.

GROWTH THROUGH YOUR TERRORS

Everyone we admire for their craft started out an amateur. Don't let your pride stop you from growing. Don't let the terror of failing hold you back. Terror is the enemy of your future, don't deny yourself and those who need you and the gifting that is within you.

In life it's not so much about what happens to you, rather it's what happens in you when life happens to you! Terrors and trials happen to everyone, never think you are on your own. Let the experiences teach you new skills and learn more about yourself. Let it be a growing experience. What the enemy meant for harm, God will turn for good, if you have the correct attitude.

When you were born, God planted seeds inside you and you need to water them and let them grow. Never let the weeds that would grow around your seeds of greatness choke your gifting. You were born for a purpose and terror is a weed that needs uprooting - not just once, but many times. Your time has come, put terror on notice, you have decided to grow!

I remember when I was asked by my Pastor years ago, to lead a service when he was preaching. I sat there on the stage - red faced and terrified, I could feel everyone staring at me. Looking at my Pastor for inspiration and comfort he said to me - probably out of pity, "It's tough at the top isn't it?" I thought, it's not tough - it's terrifying, and we are nowhere near the top!

I want you to see that you can grow through and beyond your terror, whatever your terror is. Life has a way of testing whether you really want what you are going for. Whether you are willing to pay the price to grow? Maybe it's speaking in public, writing a book, or travelling on a plane, maybe it's asking someone to marry you or starting your own business. Whatever it is that is calling you into your future, make sure you pay the price. Be prepared to fail and get ready for growth. Not everyone is up to paying the price for success - but you can. You have it in you. You were born to grow. You are not the same height, weight and size you were at the beginning of your life so don't stop growing emotionally, spiritually, intellectually and in favour with man and God.

Terror is just a barricade that is put up by the enemies of your soul to persuade you to sacrifice your gifting on the altar of fear. Push it down and stamp on this imposter. You were made to push through obstacles and not to be turned away by them. How many frustrated people have died with tremendous potential?

YOUR PATHWAY TO GROWTH

Terror won! Terror robbed them! Terror persuaded them to take the easy route, the way less travelled. Don't you be one of them. It is sad to say the cemetery is full of potential and full of dreams and vision that terror negated and neutered. Decide that you will get everything out of you that God has placed in you and that your latter days will be greater than your former days. Decide that you are going to win and not worry about what other people think. Terror is your enemy and you must overcome it, if you don't you will be constantly frustrated.

I wasted too many years being terrified and turning down opportunities to grow. Don't you do that. Let me encourage you to grow into ALL that you can be. Put your terror to death and let your dream live.

How many dreams and visions have been sacrificed in the altar of terror? You have a unique gifting that the world needs, so summon up your courage and be prepared to go through the fire of your terror to reach the people who need you on the other side of your fear.

Life is not all about you, it is about others. It's for those who might never personally thank you or appreciate you. Yet, God will reward you. He will appreciate you paying the personal price to reach, bless and encourage His children. Jesus didn't want in his flesh to pay the price, but He said, "Not my will but yours will be done!" (Mark 14:36). Follow his lead and release your gifting. Let it flow. Let it bring healing to those who are hurting. People want the real you and terror is the price. Are you willing to pay it? "Not by might, nor by power, but by my Spirit, says the Lord!" (Zechariah 4:6) You cannot do it in your flesh, but you can with God's help.

As I write this, I feel God pushing me in my back and provoking me to share this truth. You are much more than people currently see. You are worth more. The resources you need are coming your way if you will only conquer this terror. Your future can be different. You can survive a broken marriage, bankruptcy, and physical or emotional abuse. Whatever your terror is, don't let it intimidate or frustrate you. You can be it, do it and have it. Whatever 'it' God has sown in your life. You must experience the valleys of life to be able to enjoy the mountain tops. Therefore, put terror to one side, side step it and grow into what is waiting for you.

Some people are held back by the terror of someone teaching them information they didn't know. They are cocooned in a bubble of pride and it stops them learning from anyone because their cocoon has made them unteachable and therefore unreachable. Their inverted pride is often because they feel inferior and when they are given the opportunity to be the learner, rather than the teacher they really struggle. This is because they basically feel inferior and the terror for them is for that inferiority to be confirmed. This is nonsense.

Everyone can teach, and everyone can learn; however, if you won't listen and learn from others you will lose. This is a trap and a pit that has caught you like an animal in a snare. God hates pride. He hates His creation being unwilling to learn from each other. Put aside these barriers and grasp the learning opportunities that come to you.

I have learnt so much from very unusual people. People who I might not agree with very much, but I have learnt amazing truths. When you humble yourself, God will pour out His blessings and opportunities on you. Do you remember the story in 2 Kings 5, when Naaman was told to bathe seven times in the Jordan? Naaman was desperate for healing but the only true healing for him was only going to come through him humbling himself. Naaman's pride was hurt. He was angry and willing to walk away without his healing. His healing only came because he was willing to put his pride and preconceived ideas to one side and listen to those who were serving him. His servants told him his pride was holding him back and blocking his healing. It was only when he put his pride to one side and followed their instructions that God touched his terror. Are you letting the fear of not knowing the answer to everything stopping you grow? Put your pride to one side, listen and learn and you will begin to see some progress.

Many years ago, my wife Sue was employed by a major U.K. charity to promote their charity and raise funds for their work. Passing the interview and getting the job was the easy part, the hard part was going out to meet new people. She hated the very thought of it. I remember calling her at home to see if she had left for work that morning and she said she hadn't. She couldn't do it. I was so frustrated. I came home from work to see what the problem was, and I found her sitting by the radiator terrified.

However, this was an imperative moment for her. This is when she decided either to let terror win or face up to it and conquer her fear. Anybody who knows her now will testify to what happened. She put the terror to one side and with some

YOUR PATHWAY TO GROWTH

help, faced her fears and succeeded amazingly in the job. She broke through the limitations of her past and did not let terror win.

When we decide to put certain limitations on what we can accomplish, we limit what we will achieve. Don't limit your possibilities, we serve a God of the impossible. Our problem is, we spend too much time with our eyes on our limitations. Decide to upgrade your knowledge of God and His unlimited impossibilities that He has for your life. All things are possible to you when you acquaint yourself with His incredible capabilities. We serve a God who has intended you to succeed. The terror you are experiencing which is designed to keep you from your destiny, does not come from Him. Many have turned back from defeating what terrifies them unnecessarily. You do not have to be one of the many, you can be one of the few. You can grow.

Actions to help you GROW through your TERRORS!

1 Identify what terror you must overcome, so you can grow and prosper.

2 What can you do to combat these terrors? Decide, declare and agree with a friend that you will conquer these fears one step at a time.

3 Write down a pledge to do it even if you are terrified.

4 Whatever is limiting you, decide to shake it off.

5 Take your eyes off your limitations and put them on the unlimited capabilities of your God.

Quotes on Your Terrors

> "Peace I leave with you. I do not give to you as the world gives. Do not let your hearts be troubled and do not be afraid."
>
> - John 14:27 -

> "Better hazard once than always be in fear."
>
> - Thomas Fuller -

> "If the Lord be with us, we have no cause of fear. His eye is upon us. His arm over us. His ear open to our prayer. His grace sufficient. His promise unchangeable."
>
> - John Newton -

> "We fear men so much, because we fear God so little. One fear cures the other. When a man's terror scares you, turn your thoughts to the wrath of God."
>
> - William Gurnell -

> "Fear is a self-imposed prison that will keep you from becoming what God intends you to be."
>
> - Rick Warren -

CHAPTER FOUR

4

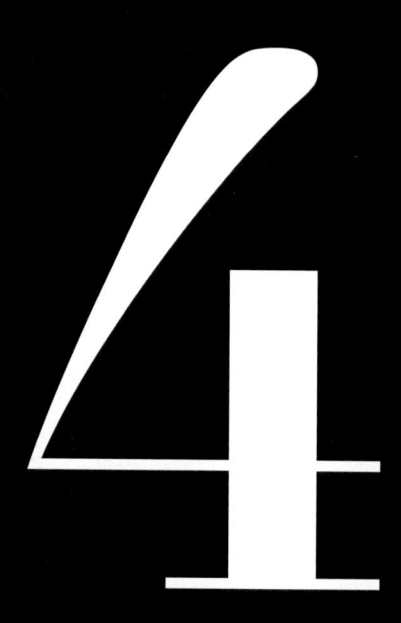

GROWTH THROUGH TRAINING AND TEACHING

WHO ARE YOUR TEACHERS?

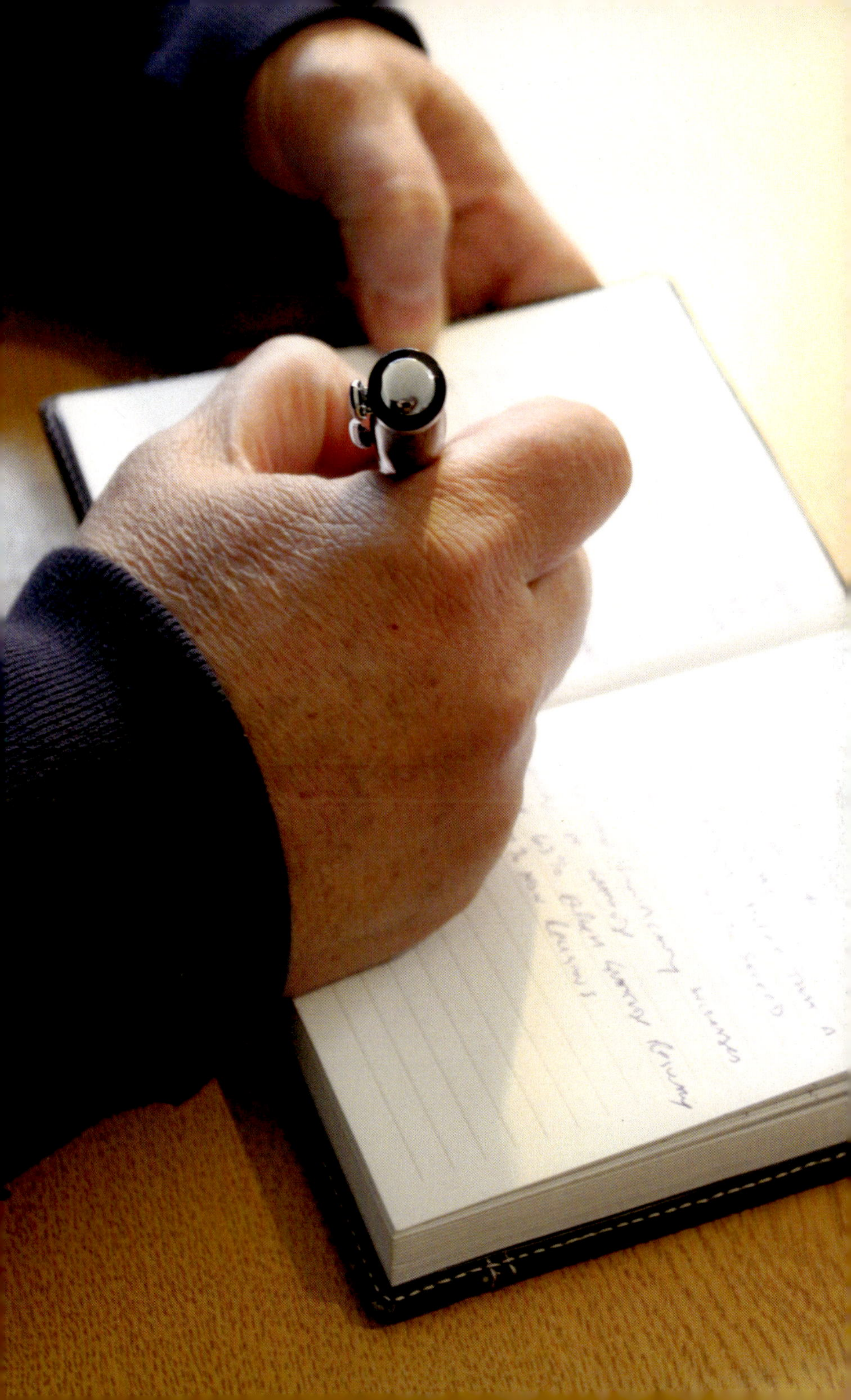

YOUR PATHWAY TO **GROWTH**

GROWTH THROUGH TRAINING AND TEACHING

Who are your teachers? Are you teachable? Bishop TD Jakes said his mother used to tell him, "Life is your teacher, make sure when you get up every morning that you go to school." Life will give you lessons for free, if you will pay attention. The lessons can be challenging, but if they help you grow, then it is certainly worth the hard work.

You can also grow by teaching in another way; teach the lessons you have learned. You learned the lesson and you grew, but you can compound your learning by teaching others the same lesson you learned. When you do this, your growth goes into overdrive.

Does being taught something frustrate you? Do you feel superior to it? If you do, you won't grow. Everyone is your teacher if you are willing to learn from them; however, if you are proud, you won't learn. Watch, listen and learn. Every book, film, experience, trauma, and every relationship you encounter is your teacher. When you decide to become a pupil, the world will teach you and prepare you for your future.

Pride will try and stop you, jealousy will try and stop you, envy will try and deny

GROWTH THROUGH TRAINING AND TEACHING

your growth. Lust will try and get you to reach for what doesn't belong to you and greed will try and distract you. Don't fall for their temptations; they are only distractions. Your future is much better than what they offer.

In certain situations, you are the teacher and in other situations you are the pupil. Wisdom is knowing the difference. If you don't learn the difference, you will miss the blessings that are intended for you. Your spouse, your superiors and your subordinates will teach you. Moreover, your contemporaries will teach you if you can get over your pride and competitiveness. What is more, your past, your mistakes and regrets will try and teach you too. They all have a part to play in building the real you – the progressive you. Every part of your past and your present helps you in your future growth.

A professional chef will use all the ingredients at their disposal to make something wholesome and beneficial. This is like an illustration of your life: each season, person and situation put together is trying to teach you and make you into the best you. Are you willing to learn? Don't be proud. Don't be insecure. Look carefully, look at every area of your life, and learn the lessons that life is trying to teach you.

A railway train takes you from A to B. It takes you from one destination to another but be sure you are on the right train. One day, a ticket inspector was examining the passengers' tickets. The inspector approached the first passenger and he concluded their ticket was for a different destination. He told the person they needed to get off at the next stop. He moved on to the next person and they also had the wrong ticket, and then the third and the fourth person were just the same. Yes, you have guessed it, the ticket inspector was the one on the wrong train. Training takes you from where you currently are to a new destination. If you choose the right train, you will arrive at a better place.

My house has a new occupant. She is called Willow and she is a Cavapoo. I bought her for my wife's birthday. Sue had wanted another dog for several years; I wasn't convinced but I ran out of excuses. Eventually, the dog duly arrived. Willow arrived looking very small, but she is growing; not only is she growing but she needs training too. This takes time and patience. There is no point having expectations that are too high. She is being trained and she is trying her best, she wants to please us, and we congratulate her with encouragement when there are small victories. We say very little when there are accidents. If you have a child or

YOUR PATHWAY TO **GROWTH**

a pet, you might know exactly what I mean!

Training needs patience. Time and patience are great warriors in your fight to learn and grow positively. God will encourage you as your training goes forward. Be patient with yourself. People are often impatient and judgemental with themselves; God is never like that. He literally has all the time in the world and eternity too. Training and learning take time – you must find the time. There is always time, you just must make it available to yourself. Earl Nightingale said, "If a person will spend one hour a day on the same subject for five years, that person will be an expert at that subject."

God doesn't rub your nose in your mistakes, as my mother used to do when we had puppies and they had accidents. If you respond and are willing to learn by the training God offers you, each day you will grow. If you are not willing, you will constantly ask yourself why you are not fulfilled and being blessed. Willow's training is a series of encouragements as she grows and adapts in our presence. As it is with her, so it is with God. He constantly encourages us to adapt to living in His presence. He is using anything and everything to train us to grow. You are under His tutelage. You are in His academy for excellence. He wants you to be all that you can be. Even His silence is telling you something. His encouragement is helping you to grow too.

Life has different levels for you to grow towards. Steps that you need to have the courage to take sometimes. Each step will take you higher. Your training is one such step. Be prepared to take a step towards living at a higher level, this is part of deciding you are going to grow.

We need to look at what barriers hinder us in devoting our time to train. For example, if one wants to become more accomplished in playing the guitar, then is the instrument within easy reach? Do we switch off the TV? Put away the computer? Make sure that at some point in the day, it's just the guitar and you? Do you inspire yourself by listening to expert guitar players? Do you have autobiographies of guitar players within reach? Are you teaching anyone the guitar and what you have learned? You have to make it easier to start training by taking away the barriers and distractions and replacing them with what I call enablers: the people, books, and instruments that enable you to train and grow.

GROWTH THROUGH TRAINING AND TEACHING

It doesn't matter what age you are or how much money you have got. Money is irrelevant. You don't need money to grow. You need a mind which has decided to grow. You don't need the right circumstances or even the right people. You are a majority of one. You are the major shareholder, the CEO of your corporation and the director of your training and travel.

People who are willing to train are hungry for more, they have an appetite to go forward. You must come to a point in your life when staying as you are is more painful than training and equipping yourself to go forward. You must decide that you are the trainee and your God is the Trainer. The investment He has placed in you is not the finished article. He needs your cooperation, He wants a partnership between the pupil and the teacher. When He sees you begin to sweat for your dream, when He sees you put yourself in the right position and put your pride to one side, sit down and learn; He has endless possibilities and opportunities waiting for you.

You need to train and be ready to capitalise on what is ahead. Study and learn and train for your future opportunities. Doors will be opened, but only training will get you through the door. Invest now and be ready for your opportunities. The difference between a dream and a goal is training. Dreaming puts you to sleep if you don't train and see your dreams awakened. Training prepares your seat for recognition and acceptance by those who can place you in your promised land. The only reason the Israelites were given the promised land was that they had experienced the training of the wilderness. Most people are not prepared to go through their wilderness training and reach their promised land. Learn to embrace the training that life will teach you. Yes, it might be hard, but persevere through your hard times.

Training tests your pride; be willing to learn. Be willing to ask questions, read books and watch DVDs. Find a master. Put yourself in the company of people who will mentor and train you. You may have to take yourself out of the company of those who have nothing to teach you and put yourself in the room with people who will train you to be all you can be. I always think the word trainee has such negative connotations; it shouldn't have. Trainees put themselves in a position to learn and to grow. They are the next master! They have put themselves in line for success. Don't let your pride stop you from crossing over to your promised land. The only difference between the trainee doctor and the surgeon is training and growth. The only difference between the professional artist and the amateur artist is training and growth and the only difference between the millionaire and the multimillionaire is training and growth. Most people initially achieve limited success in their training and immediately settle. The winners see training as a process and not a destination.

We are built to continually learn through life. Not just in our teenage years or in our twenties but through each decade. I hear someone ask, "But what about my age? Am I too old to train?" You are never too old. Moses was 80 when he confronted Pharaoh. Abraham was 75 when he left Haran and set out with his wife and family for a land he didn't know. Age is irrelevant. If God is filling your nostrils with air, then get ready to go forward. Old brains can learn new tricks.

In a study by the University of Toronto they found that older adults can perform just as well as young adults on visual, short-term memory tests. Interestingly, they found that instead of using the parts of the brain that younger people do, the older people used a different area of their brain. They found that the older brain is more resilient than what they expected. In the tests the older brain performed just as well as the younger brain. In fact, some tests showed that strategic learning may increase with age. What most experts confirm is that an older brain needs active engagement and to be continually learning.

Actions to help you GROW in your TRAINING

1 Think of a teacher that you have admired in your life? What qualities did they have?

2 What stops you from taking practical steps to grow in your learning? What can you do to change that?

3 Have you ever taken five years to become an expert in anything?

4 Are you prepared to get up earlier, stay up later or miss meals to learn? If not, why not?

5 Be attentive during your day. Look for every opportunity to learn.

GROWTH THROUGH TRAINING AND TEACHING

> Quotes on Training

"If a person will spend one hour on the same subject for five years, that person will be an expert on that subject."

- Earl Nightingale -

"The world is a university and everyone in it is a teacher. Make sure when you wake up in the morning, you go to school."

- Bishop T.D. Jakes -

"Anyone who stops learning is old, whether at twenty or eighty. Anyone who keeps learning stays young."

- Henry Ford -

"Have more humility. Remember you don't know the limits of your own abilities. Successful or not, if you keep pushing beyond yourself, you will enrich your own life-and maybe even please a few strangers."

- A.L. Kennedy -

CHAPTER FIVE

5

GROWTH THROUGH TEAMWORK

YOU MUST VALUE YOUR TEAM

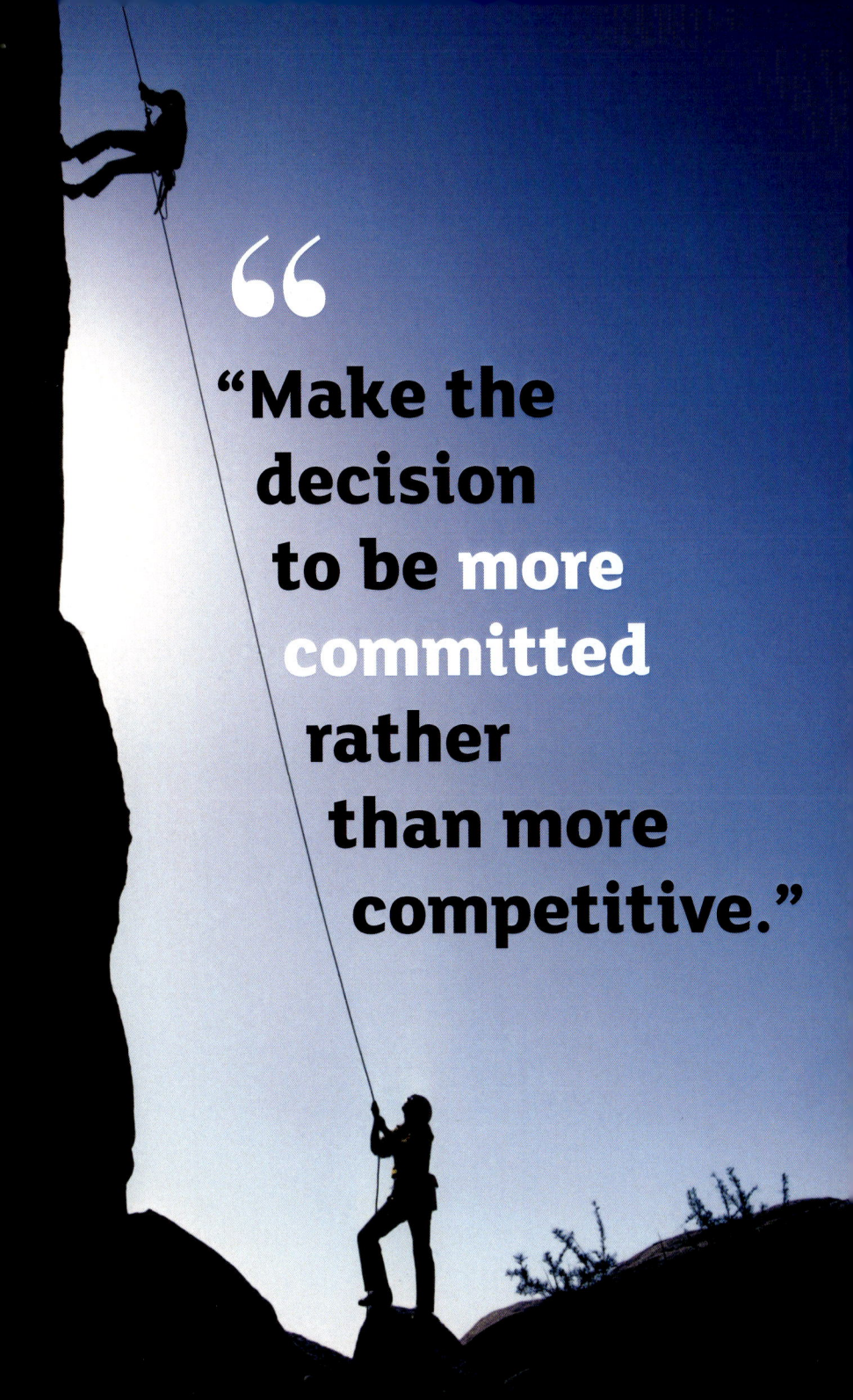

"Make the decision to be **more committed** rather than more competitive."

YOUR PATHWAY TO **GROWTH**

GROWTH THROUGH TEAMWORK

As I begin this chapter I am travelling from New Delhi to London. Sitting beside me is the other half of my dream team: my wife and co-pastor Sue. In our home church, the freedomcentre, there is another team. These people have been prepared to give us years of their lives to bring about the vision God gave us. Our own family is another team who are totally committed in loving us. There is also a team of trustees who oversee our three charities and a team who support our church financially. There is a further team who pray for us.

Without a great team you can forget your amazing dream. Without a team there is no new you. No growth. No future. So, learn to appreciate and value your team. Whether it's your spouse, children, parents or staff. Don't go forward without taking your team with you. In fact, I would say a future without your team is not a future worth having. If you can appreciate and bless your team, you will grow into even greater blessings. Greater heights. Greater blessings. You need them, and they need you. Don't sprint ahead too far and be sure to keep setting a pace that doesn't intimidate or suppress them. Get ahead, be ahead, but don't lose them. If you do, you will lose their support and they will lose the blessing of where you are taking them. Growth is not just for you; it's for the team around you. I would challenge you, if you are part of a team, by asking you this: Do you want your team to win as much as you want to win? Are you as committed to those around you winning as you are to you winning?

GROWTH THROUGH TEAMWORK

At the freedomcentre, we have endeavoured to build a strong and mature team. We truly want them to win; we want to see them grow into all they could possibly be. They sometimes frustrate us, they sometimes bless us, and they sometimes surprise us. The great thing is they are the team that God has given us. We thank God for them. We know for sure they love us, we know they have our back, we know we can frustrate them, and we know they don't always understand us, but one thing is for sure: God has given us to them and them to us. Yes, they fail, and they feel frustrated by us and we sometimes fail them, but we are in this together. We couldn't be on this journey without any of the teams that surround us. If we achieve anything significant, it's because of their support.

If we need teams, you need them too. Build people around your vision who understand, love, support and bless you. It takes time to build great teams. You will feel hurt sometimes and you will activate the wrong friendships. You will invest in those who leave you and you will feel disappointed, but it's worth the struggle to get the right people around you. Appreciate them, mentor them, seek to grow them and not just yourself. You will grow when you grow them. Pick a team who add value to your life, they will add to you and not subtract from you. Choose those who complete you and not compete with you. It takes time for them to capture your DNA and for you to trust them. Unity takes time but it's worth it. You are reading this book because of the team that surrounds me. All the different teams behind me have blessed you by their loyalty, friendship, love, financial commitment, prayers and resilience.

A story about a great team is illustrated by the experience of Proctor and Gamble when they discovered and manufactured the product known as Febreze. I will not go into the long story of how it was discovered, but simply put - it was through an employee's wife noticing that he was no longer smelling like the cigarettes he smoked every day.

He was part of one team who discovered the product. There was another team who tried to sell the product and were experiencing difficulties. Seemingly, the product was bought once and then left on the shelf in the cupboard and never used regularly. This brought in yet another team: the marketing team. They began to research why people were not buying the product. They simply couldn't find an answer. Three great teams all finding they couldn't find an answer.

YOUR PATHWAY TO GROWTH

However, the answer finally came when they interviewed one lady who was a regular user of the product and she told them she didn't use Febreze as a bad odour solver, but as a perfume to be used at the end of the clean in any room. This was like the cherry on the cake. This was the answer the company was looking for. The first team struggled to find answers, the second team struggled too, but the third team initiated the breakthrough. All three teams were part of the same company and when they worked together the answer became available. It was their unity that brought about the vast profits and sales of the multi millions. When your teams work together the results will come.

Working in unity is not always what you see because some teams are made up of competing individuals. Many years ago, I was working in sales, we sold Yellow Pages advertising. The sales people were divided up into teams and the results of the individuals in the team were known to everyone. All that you achieved – or didn't achieve – was made known and celebrated or otherwise. Pressure was put on the individual sales person to achieve the results the company were aiming for. It was a very competitive atmosphere and you were either succeeding or failing every day, every week, every month. The huge pressure to achieve results was intense.

However, this competitive atmosphere was lacking one thing. Unfortunately, it was all about comparing yourself with others. It encouraged either pride or discouragement. Bill Gates said:

"Don't compare yourself with anyone in this world. If you do so, you are insulting yourself."

The company I worked for wanted me to compare my growth with others, but they never encouraged me to compare myself with what I was capable of. If you need people to address your shortcomings, it's because you are not accountable to yourself. If someone else needs to set your standards, then you have already fallen short. You should be setting your own personal goals and objectives. Only you truly want the very best for you, so take authority over yourself before other people do. It's less painful.

God is your audience, but there will be many others who will notice your self-discipline too. A good habit is made when you decide to never let the response of other people determine the value of your contribution. People shouldn't be your barometer of success. You know when you have done your best, so receiving applause defies the point. It's whether you have achieved your very best; that is true success.

Being a great team member is when I decide I will be better this month than I was last month. I will decide to up my game, not to be better than my fellow team member but to be a better me. Please be aware, people stop growing when the price becomes too high; they will step away because it's too costly. Do you remember the rich young ruler in the Bible? He didn't want to give his cash away because it was too high a price for him to join the team (Luke 18: 18-23). Decide to pay the price that needs to be paid to reveal the real you.

Make the decision to be more committed rather than more competitive. Be focused and encourage others so that you see the aims and objectives of your team realised. Add true value to them and don't look for an immediate harvest; instead, worry more about sowing the right seed. Many team leaders motivate by giving rewards, but prizes should be given for sowing, not reaping. Sowing will bring the rewards, so concentrate on your team sowing well and the rewards will take care of themselves.

I want to remind you of the ultimate team: The Father, The Son and The Holy Spirit. Think of this commodity: The Father willing to sacrifice His Son for you and the Holy Spirit sacrificing more than two thousand years to comfort, support and fill you. Think of The Son saying,

"Not my will, but yours be done!" Mark 14:36

That's a great example of sacrificial team spirit. It's the vision of the team that counts, rather than how we feel about our own personal future. This is a team vision; the days of one-man bands are over. It's not about you, it's about what growth you can see because of your team. When we die to ourselves, we bring life to those we seek to bless. If your team is going to get the job done, sometimes they will feel deserted, rejected and hurt, but if they persevere, the world will see and benefit from the growth your team brings.

Do you have a team? You need one! Decide today to gather them around you. Pray for your team. Reward your team. Make them feel valuable and valued. They will grow despite their inhibitions, if you call them to higher ground.

YOUR PATHWAY TO GROWTH

Decide what culture your team should have. Give them candid feedback and develop them. If you do that, loyalty will follow. Celebrate the successes of the team. At the end of the day, your team wants to be successful, so make sure you point out your team's successes and reward the members publicly and privately. Pray for them, as God has brought them to you. One day, Jesus called the disciples to become part of His team; they were called from all sorts of backgrounds. They gave up businesses and they gave up a secure future because they had heard an eternal call. They didn't have any idea what the future held, but they knew growth was coming if they joined the team.

Some people will not know why they are joining your team, they will just know something significant is calling them. Be prepared for all sorts of difficulties, for trouble and even rejection. You will have a 'Judas' as well as Jesus and your 'Judas', like Jesus, will push you to your destiny. It's part of the journey, my friend. Don't be worried or concerned by it. It's all part of growing in your team. A team is made up of people who have limits and who are growing. At the beginning of their call the disciples were irritated by the children, but in the end, they were willing to give their very lives.

Your team is growing too: numerically, physically, emotionally, spiritually and in many ways. Don't get frustrated with them, wait for them to mature. They will surprise you. They will be there when you least expect it. On the other hand, beware of the times when they might disappear when you need them. Remember, there is another team who will never leave you or forsake you. They are there until the end and beyond the end of your journey. Your eternal team will take you to your reward in eternity. So, learn to have a "we did it" spirit and attitude rather than an "I did it" attitude. If you have the right attitude, your growth will multiply. You will develop growers rather than just followers.

The secret of passion is purpose. Make sure your purpose is clear, concise and making the difference for those involved and for those you are seeking to serve. Keep your purpose in view and accessible, so that people know where they are going and what they are sacrificing their lives for. Your job is to develop and make your team grow. The talents within your team will take you to the next level. So often in business, I saw team members doing fake work and not real work. They spent their energies pretending to work, instead of producing and adding value to the team. You could say that their deception was the problem, but in fact it was the team leader's fault. The team spirit was wrong, the goals were not either made plain or achievable, the training or accountability wasn't in place. The team wasn't functioning well, and ultimately it was the leader's responsibility. There needs to be direct communication from team leader to team member. Most people will work hard if their talent is being leveraged towards success. They need training. They need appreciating. They will even accept discipline if it takes them to a higher place and provokes growth in them and their family. People want to belong and desire to belong to a community that loves and appreciates them.

If you are part of a team but not the team leader at present, then decide to be the change that is needed. Encourage, support and help those in the team around you. Begin to do the right things and you will find that, as you grow, the titles and the rewards will follow you in due course. If you bring the values of the team higher, your success will go to a higher place too. Loyalty always goes to the one who provides success and growth.

One last point about building a team: never collect a losing mentality. You can have too large a team. It's a team of winners you need, not people who just want to be in the inner circle. Many people just want to be inside the rope. They want to know what's going on, but they don't particularly want to add value. On your team you need 'A' performers. I would rather have two 'A' performers than 20 people who just show up. Jesus picked 12 and invested heavily in 3 of them. He had 70 who were around, but he had levels of access and intimacy. Why would you share all you have with people who have their own agenda and won't pay the price to come with you on your journey?

Therefore, don't just build numbers; build people who are committed to you, your vision and the growth you want to see. When you are gathering a team, don't just look at references: look at them. Look at how they treat people who can do nothing for them. Look at their consistency with time management. Look at how organised their lives are. Look and see if they show a hunger to grow. Have they grown since you met them? Are they teachable or does their ego get in the way? Can they receive instruction from you? Would they serve you for free?

As a leader in the charitable sector, I must find leaders who have nothing to gain financially from serving in our team. That means it's not easy to always access the Human Resources that you need. We need an adaptable team. You need people who can turn their hands to various tasks. Some people will want to join your team because they can do one thing well, my question to them is: You can do this one thing but what else can you do? You can sing but can you type? You can administer but can you preach? You can see visions, but can you be friendly to the newcomer? Church is not dissimilar to a business. A modern

YOUR PATHWAY TO GROWTH

business needs versatile and adaptable personnel. Build a team that is versatile and flexible. No matter how small they are in numbers, make sure they are large in their capabilities. If your team is limited, you will be limited. You will only grow to the limits of the capabilities and faith of the team around you. It's ironic because often as a leader, people will accuse us of not growing quickly enough, but they don't realise that often, they are the ones limiting the very success they want.

When the little boy handed over his bread and fish in Matthew 14:13-21, he was handing over his only resource so that God would bless it. There was enough for him, but not enough for the need around him. God blessed his 'not enough,' and it became more than enough. It was his faith in Jesus (the leader) that offered the opportunity to feed the crowd. It was when the newest member of the team offered their all that the rest of the team saw a miracle. You need all your team, from the newest to the oldest, to believe and have faith in you. If they are second guessing and doubting you, they shouldn't be on the team. They will inhibit and delay your growth. So, don't ask or collect a bigger team, seek a better team. The difference between success and failure is often a great team.

In the same way a plant grows towards the sun no matter where it is placed, so do people. People are attracted to what they are exposed to. As the leader of the team, you set the pace. You set the bar and the standard. If you set low expectations, people are frustrated, the standards decline, and your team and vision are stunted. Growers need to be amongst growers. They bounce off each other and momentum is released.

Actions to help you GROW your TEAM

1 Who is on your team?

2 What is your team's DNA?

3 Is your team the correct size for your aims and objectives?

4 How flexible is your team? Are they willing to learn new skills?

5 Why are your team members on the team? Who or what are they there for? What is their motivation?

❝ Quotes on teams

"Talent wins games, but teamwork and intelligence win championships."

- Michael Jordan -

"Alone we can do so little, together we can do so much."

- Helen Keller -

"None of us are as smart as all of us."

- Ken Blanchard -

"None of us, including me, ever do great things. But we can all do small things with great love, and together we can do something wonderful."

- Mother Teresa -

"If everyone is moving forward together, then success takes care of itself."

- Henry Ford -

CHAPTER SIX

6

GROWTH THROUGH TEARS

TURN YOUR WOUNDS INTO WISDOM

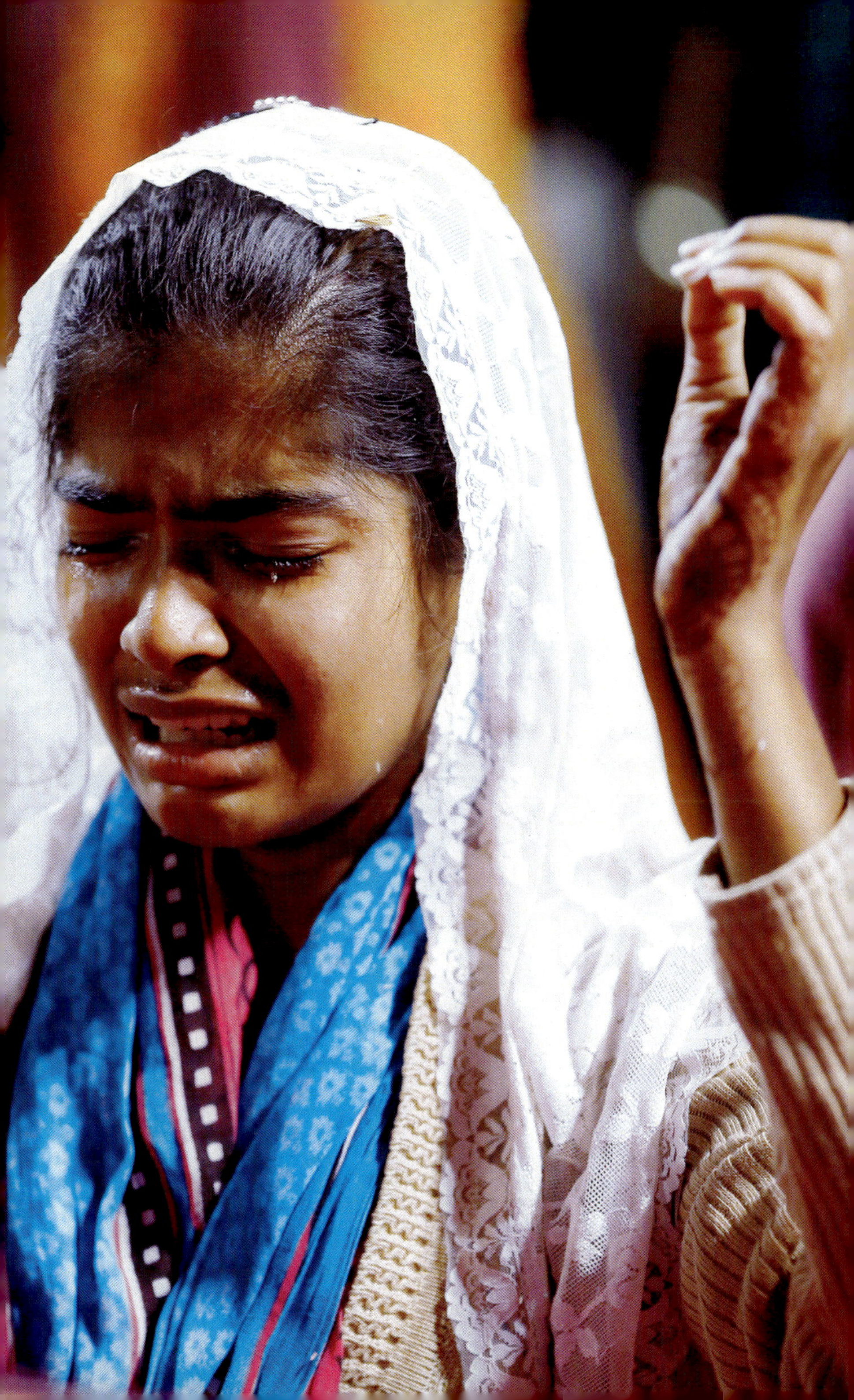

GROWTH THROUGH TEARS

Most people would like to turn back time and make different decisions. They deeply regret certain decisions, relationships and many other painful things they have gone through. The truth is, everyone would like to go back because we have all made mistakes. However, there is little point going back because, if we were able to turn back time and start again, we would simply make other decisions that we would later regret.

The apostle Paul was a dedicated opponent of the disciples and followers of Jesus. He wanted them punished and killed; they were petrified of him. When he had his Damascus Road experience and met Jesus for himself, he was full of regret. He must have wished he could have gone back and reversed the terrible punishments he gave out, but that was impossible. The truth is, if he had been able to change what he had done, he would have made other decisions that he later regretted, as he said in Romans 7:19-20:

"For the good that I will to do, I do not do; but the evil I will not to do, that I practice. Now if I do what I will not to do, it is no longer I who do it, but sin that dwells in me."

There is a lesson to be learned right here. Mistakes will occur because mistakes are inside of you. You will regret these mistakes; however, the biggest mistake is to let them control and define you. All that you have gone through – all the testing and turbulence in your life – can make you grow, if you give it the chance. Stop cursing your crisis and realise it can be a blessing in your life, if you handle it properly. The Bible says rejoice in your trials (James 1:2). It's the testing and the turbulence that gives you the opportunity to grow; they give you the signal to transition from trouble to transformation.

Some people want to escape their particularly painful situation. If their marriage gets difficult, they want out. If the job is no longer what it was, they leave. If the diet becomes hard work, they ditch it. We live in a society that says, "Whatever you do, don't suffer. Take a pill, take a loan, take a break, take it easy – just don't suffer." I have found there is growth to be experienced during these times. I have seen people grow through losing their loved ones and going through incredible mourning. I have seen people grow after losing their liberty. I have seen people grow after rejection, criticism, and when they have been ostracised or when they have lost their jobs.

Growth comes through painful and trying times. I am flying from Chennai, India to New Delhi in the North and the plane has started to experience turbulence. Do you think the captain has decided to turn back and give up the journey to the destination we are intended to arrive at? No, the plane will not turn back; it just means we need to put our seatbelts on. We can't go back because we have people to see, things to do and connections to make.

You may be going through an incredibly turbulent situation right now. It may or may not be your fault, but you are still suffering. Put your seatbelt on. Buckle up: you are going to reach the destination God has for you. You have people down the road who are waiting for the new you, the stronger you and the better you. You have connections to make for your future. I want you to know that you WILL come through this turbulence and trial and be bigger, better and still on course. Just because they left you, it doesn't mean God left you; just because your boss doesn't appreciate you, it doesn't mean God doesn't love you; and just because people are conditional with their love for you, it doesn't mean you don't have God's unconditional love.

Your testing will always stretch you. Nobody likes being stretched, but it's in the

YOUR PATHWAY TO GROWTH

stretching that you begin to be what you were meant to be. We love going to Scotland; sometimes when we are in Perthshire, we visit a glass making factory where they allow you to see the various glass objects being manufactured. I have watched in amazement, as the skilled workers apply heat to the piece of glass and begin to bend it to the shape and design they want. The glassmith applies powerful heat and then dips the glass in water. Then the heat is applied again, and the process is repeated over and over. It is when the heat is applied to the glass that it begins to bend into its intended shape. That's when the magnificence of the creation begins to show.

If you cooperate with the creator, the heat you feel in your current situation will eventually bring out your magnificence. Let the heat and the pain you feel soften you; it is temporary, so don't let it harden you. In Hebrews 3:7-8, the Holy Spirit tells us:

"Today, if you will hear His voice, do not harden your hearts as in the rebellion, in the day of trial in the wilderness..."

Therefore, do not let some turbulence turn you back or blow you off course.

Growth doesn't come easy, but it's worth having. It may seem crazy but start thanking God for who you are and where you are. Don't question why you are in your current situation. Think Growth. Pray Growth. Confess Growth. Decide Growth. Every disaster and every problem brings an opportunity. Ask yourself, what opportunity can you find in your crisis? There will be one, but you need to look for it. It's there to be found.

God wants to make the enemy pay for what you are going through and what you have come through. Think of all the struggles you have come through and you are still standing: you are here, even if you feel like you are hanging by a thread. Others haven't made it; some gave up, some turned back, and some are no longer around, but you are still here. God will promote you to the level of pain you are willing to endure. Promotion provides benefits, but it also brings pain. Ask anybody who has ever been promoted. You may receive an increase in salary and a better expense account, but the struggle is part of the job description too. Anybody who birthed anything did it through pain. You are here for a purpose, and pain is part of the purpose. Everything is going to help you grow into your purpose. You may want to cry and feel like giving up, but don't you dare give up! Not when God promises your latter years will be greater than your former years. You are coming through and you will be stronger if you decide you will use the tears, the turbulence and the trials positively. If you want to see the mountain top, you will have to endure the valley. In fact, every successful leader you see standing on the mountain top, is standing on their failures rather than their failures being over them. Put every circumstance under your feet and move upwards.

I heard John C Maxwell say that in every trial and struggle that you go through you need to:

- **Review it**
- **Reflect on it**
- **Recover from it**
- **Rearrange your life because of it**
- **Recharge your batteries because of it.**

Don't suppress your feelings and bury the tears and the pain. Review what happened and reflect on it. Decide during that time of reviewing and reflection, that you will recover. Your life is recoverable, no matter what the current circumstances say. You will probably have to rearrange some parts of your situation, but your story is not finished. Decide to do what you must do to grow out of your pain and be stronger.

I have often seen illness devastate families. If anything brings tears, turbulence and trials, it's illness. You can somehow get through financial problems and relationship breakups, but illness can be critical. It can literally kill you. It can be final. It leaves a mark that you can't often erase. You wonder, "Why? Why me? Why them? Why us?" The more acute the illness, the bigger the trial. The crazy and mind-boggling thing is, I have seen people grow through such trials, whereas I have seen others diminish.

I believe that this happens because the people who have grown have held onto the truth that is larger than the lie of the illness. The pain comes like an uninvited guest late at night. You didn't ask for it, you don't deserve it, but still it arrives. However, you have a choice in this moment: do you wear the illness like a cloak of darkness, or do you decide that whatever happens, God will get some glory out of this uninvited guest?

YOUR PATHWAY TO GROWTH

I have seen both reactions. Some never get over their self-pity and that is understandable. However, I have seen others decide to grow. They will not let the tears, turbulence and the trials of life stop them on their growth journey. They feel pain, but they go forward anyway. It's a courageous decision, but it has tremendous rewards. There is a new promised land waiting for the brave ones who find the courage and start the journey. Everything is coming against them, sometimes it seems even God is against them, but they persevere anyway, and they get their rewards. That's growth at its finest. Nobody will understand the journey you have been on, but you will, and it will be worth it. You will see growth that others only dream of. They will wonder, "Why you? Why did you get to go to such a place? Why do you get the blessing?" You will know it's because you chose life rather than death. You chose to go forward rather than stay put. You chose growth over defeat.

If you should find yourself in a critical situation, can I encourage you to take each day at a time? Maybe even in a minute or an hour at a time. The devastation is real. Don't try and deny your situation, but recovery is possible. You are still here. That means God has a plan. As incredible as it sounds, that plan is to prosper you, give you a hope and a future. You haven't got the blessing yet; it's still to come and it will be a surprise to you. It may feel like it's a thousand miles away, but to God it's the next thing on his agenda, but you will have to grow into it.

The bad news is there are giants you will have to conquer to inherit this promise. The good news is, God is on your side and because of that fact, victory is already yours. You must occupy the ground ahead of you. Go towards the victory and leave the defeat behind. It may be a death of a loved one, a business failure, a broken marriage, a dream that has died. Whatever it is, God is not finished with you. If he was finished, you would not have woken up this morning.

God is ready to show you your future. Get ready! It will be bigger and better than you currently think. Think big. Think better. Think growth. That's the plan for your life. Do not let your enemy persuade you otherwise. God brings life out of death, light out of the darkness and he brings the truth out of lies. He makes a way when there is no way. That's your God. Don't underestimate Him. Your tears, trials and turbulence are imposters who come into your life to try and persuade you to give up. Decide to grow and the good times are ahead of you.

Some people have been left behind, rejected and disowned, and often people have connected with the wrong person and been deeply betrayed. What I have frequently seen in these situations is after all the pain, rejection and the betrayal, the wronged person eventually goes back to fish in the same pond they got hurt in. We can question, "Have they learned nothing? Have they forgotten the suffering they went through? Why do they do that? Why do we do that?" The simple answer is, we are attracted to what we are exposed to. We think there is only one pond. We think that's our place to fish. We think we don't deserve any other place to go to. We become our worst enemy.

As the saying goes: birds of a feather flock together. You see, what you have constantly been around is what you think you are. If you are God's child, you are royalty. You are an eagle, not a chicken. Part of the reason you were rejected was because you were different. People reject what is different and they don't like being challenged. Who you really are can make people jealous and feel inferior; you can actually make others do crazy things. They will leave you and betray you, rather than come up to the level you live at.

Fishing and where you choose to fish is important. You mustn't go fishing where you might catch trouble, pain and rejection. The truth is, if you hang around with the wrong people long enough, they will seem attractive. The Bible is quite emphatic in 2 Corinthians 6: the Christian life should be lived in wide-open spaces. Living in small places makes you small. You need to live expansively and if you do, you will expand. Who you choose to partner with will either enlarge you or diminish you. If you have been through trials, turbulence and tears, can I gently advise you to not go back to the same pond? Have some time out, lick your wounds and decide to learn some lessons. There is nothing for your future self in the errors of the past. You can learn from your past, but why repeat the same errors? Only a fool repeats the same behaviour and expects a different result.

You deserve better. You need a better circle. If you are the smartest person in the room, you are in the wrong room. You need to look up, not down. That means gathering the courage you will need and stop mourning the familiar. Stretch yourself and you will grow. Let your trial teach you and reveal to you the hearts of others, but most importantly your own heart. What is the need inside of you that attracts the wrong type? Whatever that void is, it needs to be filled. Whatever condition you have needs healing. Lick your wounds, apply the right teaching to your deepest and private thoughts and let yourself grow. If you don't grow out of your position, condition and situation you will fall back to the beginning, where the whole process will begin again. God says that's not your future. You cannot hold

YOUR PATHWAY TO GROWTH

hands with your past. Hate and love; trust and mistrust; loyalty and disloyalty: these opposites can't hold hands. If you insist on going back to fish in the same pond for friends, for marriage partners or for business partners then you will go back into the similar trial, turbulence and testing you have already experienced.

People will be patient and loving when you fall into hard times. However, their grace will begin to wear thin when you repeatedly go back to the same pit you fell in. They want to see you learn and grow from your experience. Growth is moving upwards when life is seeking to tear you down. God's momentum is upwards for you. He wants to take you up, not down. Your previous experience will try and draw back; you must resist that inclination. The inclination is there because it has a hold of the part of you that wants the familiar. Familiarity is not your real friend. Growth beckons you to come out of your trial by taking hold of your future by the scruff of the neck. If your trial is going to teach you anything, it needs to call you forward and that will be a new 'present' for you to enjoy. You will never be the same person after the trial you go through. However, you will be a better person if you decide to grow during the process and choose the opportunities to grow.

Actions to help you GROW through your TEARS:

1 What lessons have you learned from your past? Have you dealt with them? If so, leave your past behind and decide to move on.

2 What trials are you currently facing? How can you overcome them? Decide to stop asking God to remove you from it but ask Him to take you safely through it.

3 Once you are out of the trial, then stay out. Don't go back to your old habits or friends.

4 Living in the new present is a gift from God.

5 Learn the lesson well and keep moving forward.

GROWTH THROUGH TEARS

> Quotes on trials, testing and turbulence

"A gem cannot be polished without friction, nor a man perfected without trials."

- Lucius Annaeus Seneca -

"For the Lord your God is He who goes with you to fight for you against your enemies, to give you the victory."

- Deuteronomy 20:4 -

"Trials teach us what we are, they dig up the soil, and let us see what we are made of."

- Charles Spurgeon -

"Turn your wounds into wisdom."

- Oprah Winfrey -

"There is no education like adversity."

- Disraeli -

CHAPTER SEVEN

7

GROWTH THROUGH TEXTBOOKS

ALWAYS HAVE A BOOK ON THE GO

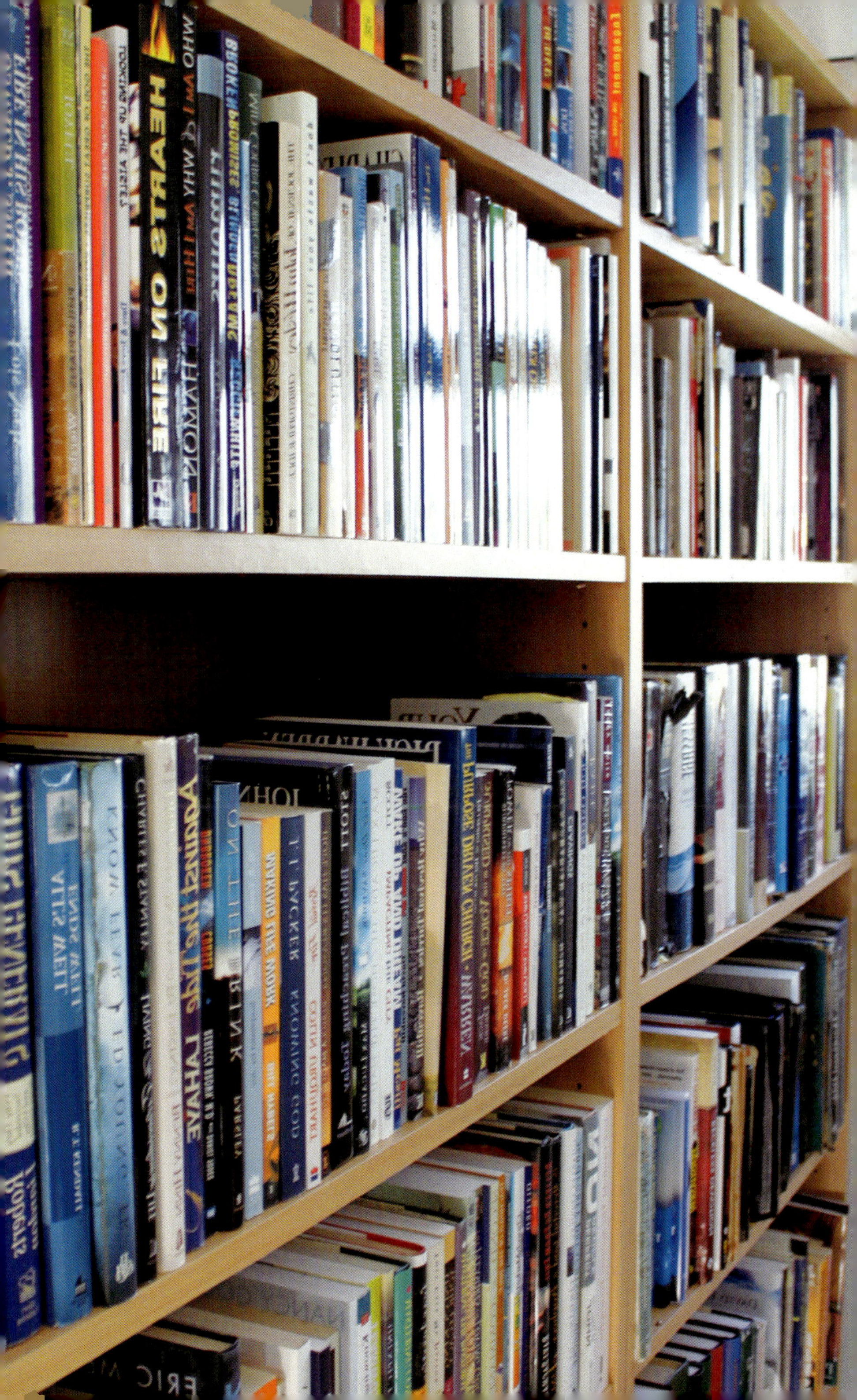

YOUR PATHWAY TO **GROWTH**

GROWTH THROUGH TEXTBOOKS

It is great that you have reached chapter seven in our growth journey. You are obviously an avid reader. I love books too. Isn't it amazing that books are still here, but records and vinyls are mostly gone? If you were to come to my office, you would see my walls lined with books. Some I have read twice, some only once and some I haven't read at all. The truth is, I just love to see them there. One day, I may get around to reading all of them; until then, they look good on my shelves.

Some authors are better leaders, preachers and teachers than they are authors, and vice versa. Some have great stories to tell, however they don't quite communicate correctly. On the other hand, some have small stories which they somehow develop into blockbusters. Learn to love books if you can. They will help you grow. Someone once said: Where you are in five years will largely depend on who you meet and what you read. I believe that. Meeting Jesus is on the top of my list and the Bible is at the top of my reading list. Think of the people who have gone before you and the lessons they can teach you. They may have gone through exactly what you are going through and some of them may be less gifted than you in certain areas, yet they made a huge success of their lives. They will tell you how to do it if you will invest the time to read their stories.

Some may have failed, others succeeded, but they all have lessons to teach you. Are you willing to learn?

Get into the habit of reading every day; always have a book on the go. Learn to have a book with you, so that you can redeem the time that is so often wasted. We can waste time waiting for appointments, at airports, train stations and bus terminals. 'Non-growers' fill their minds with anything and everything. A grower, however, is determined to use any available time to capitalise the minutes and hours that others waste. If you use your time wisely, you won't be as frustrated when waiting for that appointment or person. Life is far too short to waste. 'Killing time' is not a phrase that a person wanting to grow should use; time is too precious. Reading is a very worthwhile and productive habit. It will make you grow almost without you realising it. Don't read rubbish, read quality instead. Read encouraging autobiographies and books about history. I must admit I love autobiographies – my wife says it's because I am nosey. Maybe that's truer than I care to admit, but I find it so encouraging to realise that I am not the only one who struggles. It's comforting to know that others have struggled too, and it's inspiring to learn that if they succeeded, I can too.

Sometimes leaders, preachers and teachers give the impression that they 'have it all together'. However, we all know that deep down that this is just not true. The best books are the ones where the leaders and the teachers portray their honesty. Yet the writer must be careful not to 'cast pearls before swine'. In other words, you must be wise with what you tell and to whom, however they must never give the impression that they have grown into some sort of perfection. If the most prolific writer in the New Testament can say, "the things I would like to do I don't do, and the things I don't want to do I do," then the rest of us can be real too. I don't know what Paul was doing, but let's thank him for his honesty.

Therefore, choose good books and you will grow – spiritually, emotionally and materially. Your family will thank you for taking God's word seriously. Be a man or a woman of the Word of God and safeguards will be placed inside you that no other book imparts in the same way. It will supercharge your growth and it must come first. Don't read every book but be sure to read the book of books: The Bible. Intellectualism can never replace spiritually. I would rather be a fool in people's eyes and know God's word intimately, than have all the knowledge that man can write and not know the God who created me.

YOUR PATHWAY TO **GROWTH**

How many books have you read or listened to in the last year? If President Bush could read 186 historical and autobiographical books in two years, when serving as President of the United States, then can we read more than 4 books per year- that is what the average person reads. We can all find the time, so redeem it wisely. Decide what time of the day is good for you and keep to it.

I find it's best for me to read earlier in the day. My mind is sharp and responsive, I soak more up, and I am more focused. Other people prefer later in the day and some before retiring. Find time and decide that good textbooks are your friends and not your enemies. Let them train you. They will take you places you have never dreamt of. They will give you riches that you have never imagined. They will build you up when you most need it. Growth comes from reading text, so don't deny yourself that ingredient in your journey towards a better future.

Some books are life changing. I remember when I was in my twenties reading a book by an Anglican vicar called David Watson. The book was simply called 'Discipleship.' This great book changed my walk with God. I transformed from being a person who had simply made the decision to believe in God to becoming a true disciple that wanted to give and contribute more. I realised that I could amount to more, I could give more, and I could contribute more. I could sow my whole life rather than waste the seeds that God had put in me.

Another book that I found life changing was by Mahesh Chavda. Mahesh is one of the gentlest and grace filled men that my wife and I have ever met. He has seen the most amazing miracles, yet he remains humble. When we see him, I fall in love with Jesus more. My favourite book by him is called, 'Watch of the Lord'. It taught me about soaking in God's presence. It taught me about the value of prayer and fasting and spending nights of prayer with others seeking God. We had a season in our lives when Sue and I hosted 'Watches' every Friday evening. Eternity will reveal all that was accomplished during that significant time. We know it certainly helped to give us the courage and guidance that we needed to birth the freedomcentre. It was a tool that God used in our lives to encourage us and enable us to connect with our spiritual father, Bishop TD Jakes.

Another favourite author is John Maxwell. His leadership books are incredibly good and have taught me a huge amount; my favourite book by Maxwell is probably 'The 21 Irrefutable Laws of Leadership'. He discusses the different laws to live your life and how to lead those you are responsible for.

GROWTH THROUGH TEXTBOOKS

Robin Sharma is another great author, best known for his best seller 'The Monk who sold his Ferrari'. He has published many other books including, 'Megaliving', 'Who will cry when you die?' and 'The 5am Club'. I have enjoyed and benefited from all his books.

I love Joseph Prince, and his book, 'Let Go Life', is a great help if you suffer from anxiety and stress and want to discover a way through. Brian Houston is honest and real and his book on leadership is called 'Live Love Lead'; it is tremendous. Myles Munroe was a great writer and his books have really benefited me: 'In Pursuit of Purpose' is amazing and another favourite is 'The Principles and Power of Vision'.

Joyce Meyer writes about real life; she brings real life's issues into focus and helps you navigate through them. She has published many books, but some of my favourites are, 'Making Good Habits', 'Change Your Words, Change Your Life' and 'Living Beyond Your Feelings'.

Darlene Zchech wrote a brilliant book called 'The Art of Mentoring', where she challenges leaders to raise the next generation with love and grace. It's well worth investing in.

Charles Swindoll is a fantastic writer. His books are written with such warmth and insight. His book on Paul, 'A Man of Grace and Grit!', is amazing.

Stephen Covey, Zig Ziglar, Peter Drucker, Norman Vincent Peale, Smith Wigglesworth, Bishop TD Jakes, RT Kendall and David Yongi Cho are all authors of brilliant books to inspire the reader.

They are my favourites, but you will have your own preferences that attract and benefit you. Discovering the authors and the books you prefer is all part of your growth journey. You will grow as you dedicate yourself in reaping what they have sown in their writings.

I hope I have inspired you in some way to seek growth through books. You can buy a book for as little as a few pounds, dollars or whatever currency you use. Never begrudge the cost of a book. If you can learn great wisdom from someone's life for such a small sum, it's a great investment. It has cost them a small fortune to learn what they are teaching you, so don't resent paying whatever amount. The truth to be gleaned from these books will be well worth it. Some people find it easier to read than others – if that's you, then persevere. You might even want to buy audiobooks which you can listen to while you are driving or travelling. So many people measure their physical activity by how many steps they take or miles they have run or walked. That's brilliant if you are keen to keep physically fit and we all should. How about tracking your reading in a similar way? How many pages in a day? How many chapters in a week? How many books in a month and a year? Have you read the whole Bible? Try it in a year with a Bible planner! It's perfectly possible. Quite easy in fact. I always imagine meeting a biblical author in Heaven and trying to explain to them why I never quite got around to reading their book!

In conclusion, let's get reading if you are serious about growing. It's just like exercising your body. You brain is a muscle and it needs exercising. Start slowly but deliberately. If you must read the same page several times, so be it. It will come slowly but growth will happen.

Actions to help you GROW through BOOKS

1 What was the last book you read? Why did you read it? What did you learn?

2 Do you read the Bible? Be honest, how often do you read it? Why do you think that's the case?

3 Who are your favourite authors? Why?

4 Set yourself a target of doubling your reading. If you don't read, set yourself a target of reading a book a month.

5 Read thoughtfully, take notes and annotate.

GROWTH THROUGH TEXTBOOKS

> Quotes about reading books

"Outside of a dog, a book is a man's best friend."

- Groucho Marx -

"You cannot open a book without learning something."

- Confucius -

"You can never get a cup of tea large enough or a book long enough to suit me."

- C.S. Lewis -

"The Bible is the book of my life. It's the book I live with, the book I live by, the book I want to die by."

- N.T. Wright -

"The Bible is no mere book, but a living creature, with a power that conquers all that oppose it."

- Napoleon -

CHAPTER EIGHT

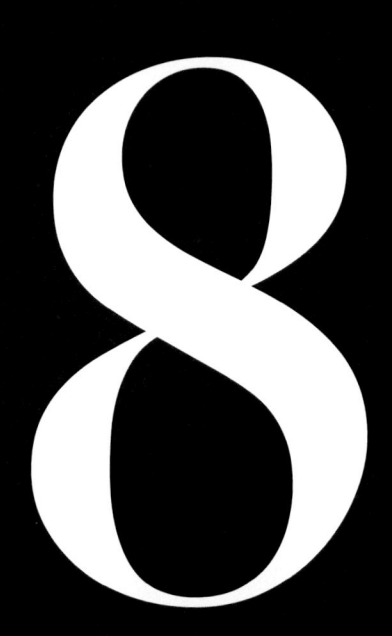

8

GROWTH THROUGH BEING THANKFUL

SAY THANK YOU!

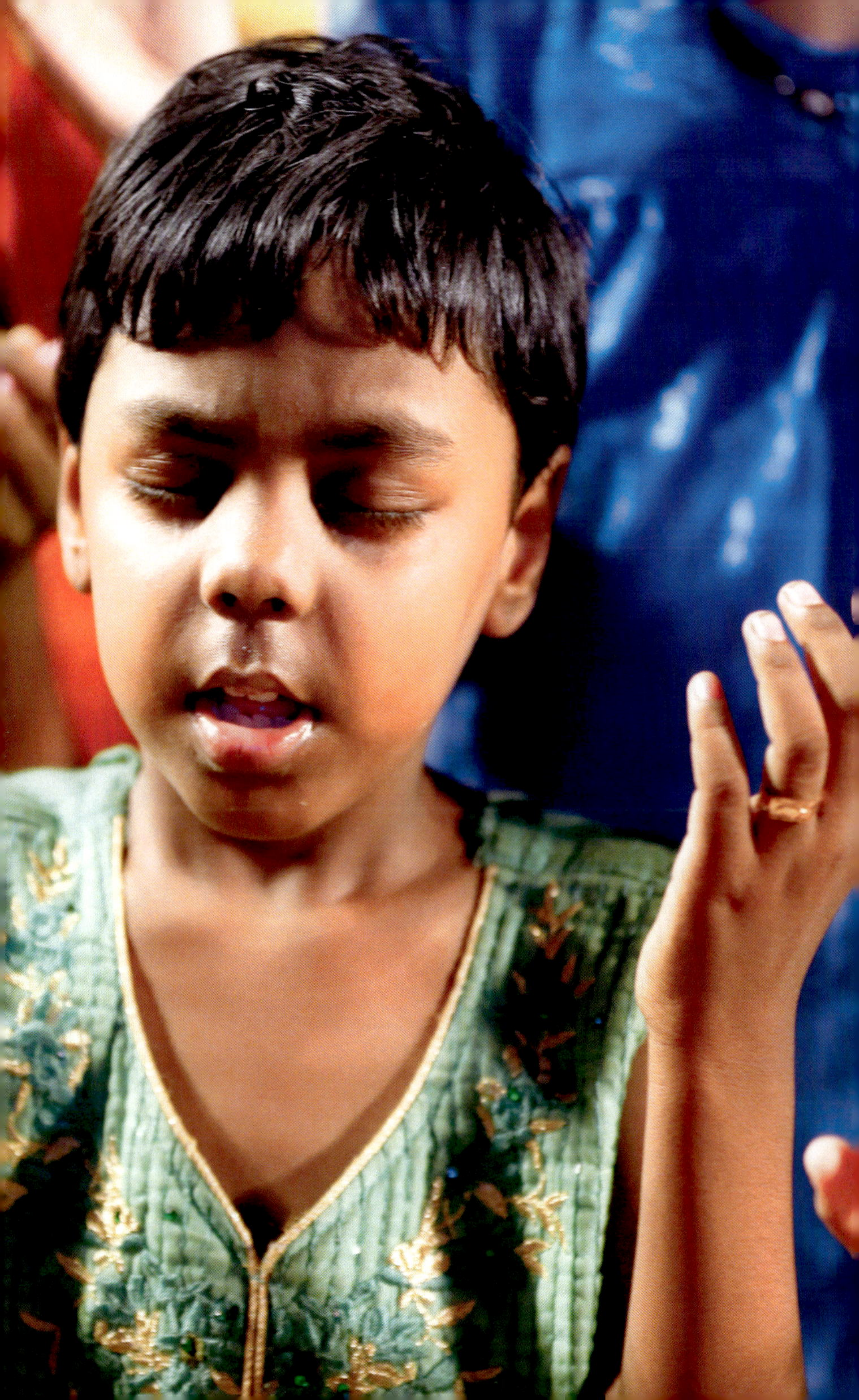

YOUR PATHWAY TO GROWTH

GROWTH THROUGH BEING THANKFUL

If you want to help make a person feel valuable, all you must do is say thank you! Some people struggle to say thanks – this is prideful, so don't be one of them. When my wife and I travel, I always try and learn the word 'thank you' in the language of the country we are visiting.

- In Tamil it's, *nandre*
- In Malay it's, *terima kasih*
- In Filipino it's, *salamat*
- In Malawi it's, *zikoma kwambiri*
- In Germany it's, *danke dir*
- In Hindi it's, *dhanyavaad*
- In France it's, *je vous remercie*
- In Spain it's, *gracias.*

They all sound different, but the meaning is the same and the reaction is the same. People are thrilled that you have gone to the trouble of learning their word for 'thank you'.

Learn to be grateful for the big and small things. Someone is fighting in hospital for the life you take for granted; someone else is struggling to pass exams to get the

GROWTH THROUGH BEING THANKFUL

degree you found easy. Another person would love the husband/wife you have and might be struggling with. Someone else would count themselves highly blessed and favoured to have your home/job/car or kids, for example.

Stop being ungrateful for your circumstances. It could be a lot worse, and maybe it will get a lot worse if you don't decide to say thank you. Growth comes from appreciating everything you have. When you learn to be thankful for all the positive things that you have, then the negative is put into perspective.

I love that the United States of America have Thanksgiving Day. Every November on the fourth Thursday, they take time to be thankful. It originated as a harvest festival celebrated by the Pilgrims after their first harvest in October 1621. It became a national holiday to give thanks and praise to God. Giving thanks is not just a single day event however, it's an every-day opportunity. Decide each day who you will be thankful for and what you will be thankful for. If you need to, make a list of who and what you are grateful for.

In Ephesians 5:19-20, Paul says, "Sing and make music in your heart to the Lord, always giving thanks to God the Father for everything!" That means the negative as well as the positive. That means anywhere and everywhere. If you don't think that is possible, then picture Jesus in Luke 22, sitting around a table with His disciples. In a short amount of time, He will be betrayed by one of them and He will be sent to trial. He wouldn't be found guilty of anything, yet he will be sent to His death – a horrific death. These are His circumstances. In this situation, what does He do? He gives thanks to His Father for the food before Him. Imagine the circumstances and ask yourself, would you be thanking God for food at this time? Somehow, I would struggle to think clearly, far less declare thankfulness. If you watch carefully in Scripture, when Jesus gave thanks to His Father, blessings always followed.

Let's imagine another scene. Lazarus has died, and four days have passed. He was dead and buried and Jesus wept. Then in John 11:41-44, Jesus gave thanks to His Father who would hear His prayer, and when He did, Lazarus resurrected from the grave.

Picture the feeding of the five thousand in Matthew 14:13. Just before the multitudes were fed, the sick people were being healed, but then they began to get hungry – they had no food and nowhere to go. What did Jesus do? He gave thanks for the little He had so that God could create an abundance.

YOUR PATHWAY TO **GROWTH**

You are spiritually growing when you learn to thank God in everything. Every obstacle you face contains an opportunity to grasp. Your obstacle is giving you an opportunity to overcome and become stronger. Thank God for your opportunity. The door of opportunity will take you to the next level. We all want to be bigger, better and stronger, but we need to realise our current circumstances are giving us that opportunity. Thank God for the opportunity to be more. Transformation has a price, so be prepared to pay for it. Be thankful that you are being given the opportunity to grow. The traumas of life can be stepping stones to take you across to a new place. Growth is never cheap; God will charge you to change you. The new you must be a thankful you. When you enter God's presence, enter with thankfulness. Don't saunter in casually but go into the Holy of Holies with a gratitude attitude.

If you want to go to the next level, the higher level, then thank those who are with you where you are now. I have known some people who forget where they have come from. If they get promoted for example, they 'burn' those left behind and if they achieve success, they immediately 'move on' from those deemed less successful. Don't be one of those who forget to honour those people with gratitude. You might not need them right now, but one day you may need them, and you don't want to burn the bridges that you might need to cross.

The truth is, if you learn to be thankful for every situation, you will learn to be happy in every situation. When we focus on the positive, we hardwire our brain to begin to see the benefit of what we are enjoying or enduring. Every situation we find ourselves in can teach us to serve and savour. There is a mission for you, if you will look up instead of down.

I met a housekeeper in Chennai, and she was an incredibly happy person. I asked her why she was so happy. I imagined that she had a monotonous and mundane job, but she saw it differently. She was energised by the opportunity of her work. Her mission was to please people by making their room clean and tidy. She would do little and thoughtful things to personalise your room, such as making animal shapes out of hand towels, and she was positive and thankful for the opportunity to serve. In fact, when I asked her what her name was, so I could review her excellent service on Trip Advisor, she told me to mention her boss because she was so thankful to her for the position she had. She was a smart lady, and she will go far because she is intent on growing and using thankfulness to take her to the next level.

GROWTH THROUGH BEING THANKFUL

How thankful you are will determine what level you will rise to. When I say 'level', I don't necessarily a financial level, a promotion or a new house or job. I am talking about a new level of enjoying the circumstances you are in. If you think of Nelson Mandela, Mahatma Gandhi or any other hero and game changer, these people were appreciative of the smallest parts of their lives. The following quote illustrates it well:

"We are so often caught up in our destination that we forget to appreciate the journey, especially the goodness of the people we meet on the way. Appreciation is a wonderful feeling – don't overlook it!" Anon.

Learn not to be jealous, intimidated or threatened by others. Teach yourself to value their gifting and be thankful that they are in your life and they are made in the image of the Father. If they are bringing poison into your situation then question their access to you, but if they have legitimate rights in your life then look for what is positive and valuable. Thank God for your differences – life would be very boring if we were all the same. We all value God the Father, God the Son and God the Holy Spirit. Why? Because they are different. They bring a different perspective and disposition to how you are loved by God.

When you decide that you will be thankful and appreciative, people will begin to reflect positively on how you are treating them. People appreciate being appreciated. You do, and they do too. You love the person who loves you. You appreciate the person who appreciates you. You thank the people who thank you. You reflect what is projected onto you. You are literally a mirror to those around you, as they are to you.

Focus on being interested in others. Offer them encouragement and help in their pursuits. If you do, they will begin – sometimes slowly – to help you in your pursuit. We live in a world where everyone is tearing around, trying to get ahead of the crowd. They are like rats trying to keep ahead of the pack. Even if you get ahead and keep ahead, you are still a rat. When you learn to be interested in others sincerely, you will be raised to a higher level. You will thrive when you look around and decide you can make a difference and be the positive difference that is needed in a company, a church, a university, a medical practice or wherever you are placed at this moment.

We met a taxi driver in Singapore who was driving us from the airport into the city. I began to ask him about his job; I can still hear his thankful voice. He was grateful for his job, where he worked 12 hours a day, 7 days a week, with little or no holidays. Why was he grateful? He had a job, he had money and he was physically fit. What would happen if he wasn't well or couldn't work for any reason? I hate to think. I reckon it would be the attitude of gratitude and thankfulness that would keep him well and take

YOUR PATHWAY TO GROWTH

him to the next level. Meeting him reminded me that we need to be thankful for what we have, because if we are not, then we probably won't be thankful for what is coming.

The opportunity to serve people brings joy. People sometimes struggle to show gratitude; they don't realise it is toxic if they are not grateful. Keep yourself at a higher level. Operate from above and don't venture down to the level of those who are ungrateful. Change doesn't come easily, but it's worth having. Make yourself your own hero. Be pleased with yourself. Be content and grateful for you. Jesus died for you! Why wouldn't you be pleased and fulfilled with you? The new, changed you, the growing you, will be a happier companion for you to have on the journey of life. Finally, why not start a 'Thankful Journey'. Each day choose five things you are thankful for in your life. Write them down – the very act of writing them will seal your gratitude for them. There is so much in our lives to thank God for. If you are struggling to think of something right now, then start with the breath in your lungs. Thank God for the air you breathe. Someone somewhere is fighting for the air you are breathing so easily. Thank God for your family, your extended family, your friends, your next-door neighbour or whoever you relate to. Be thankful for clothes, for food, for love, for anyone and everyone who has impacted your day positively. When you start to write them down, you will have far more than five and you will be strengthening the positivity in your mind.

Become grateful day by day and you will grow.

Actions to help you GROW through being THANKFUL

1 Do you find it easy to say thanks?

2 Would your peers see you as a person who is thankful for what you have?

3 Are you grateful to be you? If not, why not?

4 Decide to say thanks and show gratitude for every little act of kindness or service.

5 List three things that you are thankful for. Give God thanks for something every day.

Quotes on Thankfulness

"**Be thankful for what you have; you'll end up having more. If you concentrate on what you don't have, you will never, ever have enough.**"

- Oprah Winfrey -

"**Feeling gratitude and not expressing it is like wrapping a present and not giving it.**"

- William Arthur Ward -

"**I am thankful for every moment.**"

- Al Green -

"**No duty is more urgent than that of returning thanks.**"

- James Allen -

"**I would maintain that thanks are the highest form of thought and that gratitude is happiness doubled by wonder.**"

- G.K. Chesterton -

CHAPTER NINE

9

GROWTH THROUGH THOROUGHNESS

GIVE IT YOUR VERY BEST

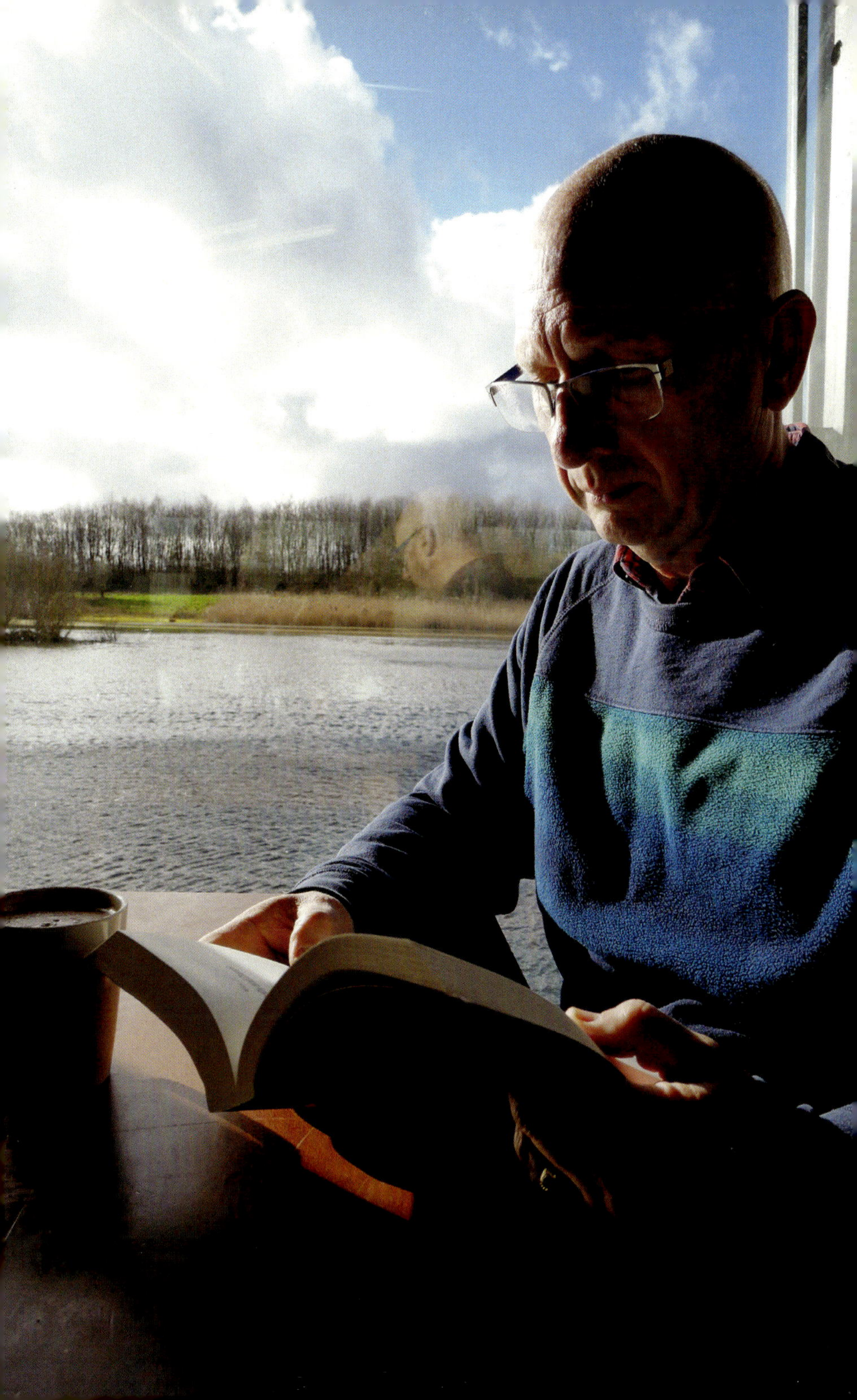

YOUR PATHWAY TO **GROWTH**

GROWTH THROUGH THOROUGHNESS

Many people aren't very good at being thorough. People left to their own devices tend to do just enough to keep their boss off their case and just enough to make a living or a profit. If you want to remain static in life, then don't be thorough. However, if you want to be in the winner's enclosure, if you mean to be ahead of the pack and get the promotion, or you want your business to succeed, then make the commitment to be thorough.

Decide to be a 'completer' finisher. So many people make a start but give up, whereas others start well but don't give it their best – they become mediocre. They do a bit here and a bit there. However, you can decide to be thorough. If someone asks you to do something, do it – thoroughly. Don't do it half-heartedly by only giving a piece of yourself to your job, marriage, church, ministry and friendships; give your all. Be thorough, focused and committed.

James Allen said this:

"Thoroughness consists in doing little things as though they were the greatest things in the world."

There is a lack of respect for the little assignments of life. People often see the small tasks as having little or no importance. It seems they save themselves for a

GROWTH THROUGH THOROUGHNESS

task which is worthy of their considerable talent. This is simply nonsense. You find everything out about someone when they are assigned a small task. If they take it seriously and do it to the best of their ability, then you have someone who can be trusted with a greater responsibility. If, however, they don't take it seriously – as if it is beneath them – then it tells you their mentality. Thoughtlessness, carelessness, and laziness are so common that you must not only avoid these characteristics yourself, but you have to weigh up whether those around you have them too. If you put your whole mind to whatever comes to hand and you do it thoroughly, you need to have no fear of your future, for there are so many who are careless, negligent and lazy that the services of the thorough man or woman will always be in demand.

Sue and I refurbished our present home, which is a 17th century barn, many years ago. At the time, we employed several tradesmen to work on it. What time has revealed is the tradesmen who were thorough and the ones who were not. Some cut corners and didn't perform to their best. Years later, it still annoys us when we go to use something or look at a feature and we see the imperfection of something not done to its best. Of course, the worker was able to do it right, but they just didn't choose to. They gave less than their very best. I have often thought what would have happened if the architect had decided to work to that standard. Walls would have been out of place and the positioning of rooms and facilities would not have fitted together. It was because the architect worked to a higher standard and gave his very best that the house came together as it did.

You cannot serve well without focus. Most people's minds are all over the place. They are thinking about what they are doing later, what they did earlier, who they are seeing and when they are seeing them, instead of focusing on the task at hand. They lack focus and then mistakes are made, and people are let down.

Sue and I were travelling one day; we asked the bellboy to take responsibility for our cases and deliver them to our taxi. We also asked the taxi driver to liaise with the bellboy to receive delivery of our cases and off we went to the airport. However, when we started to unload, the two cases were missing. The cases they had taken responsibility for weren't there; neither the bellboy nor the driver were efficient enough. Their lack of thoroughness made it necessary to make two journeys to the airport that morning.

If you want to grow, if you want promotion, if you want to be thought of as better

YOUR PATHWAY TO **GROWTH**

in any way, decide to be thorough. It will reward you. You will feel better about yourself. You will rise above those people who don't follow through. Instead, you will have a spirit of excellence because you will have been conscientious in all you say and do. If you will dedicate yourself to your craft, then the self-fulfilment you will experience in being a master in your area of skill will be amazing.

Anybody and everybody may settle for less, but if you will take it to a much higher level you will shine like a star. It doesn't matter if you are a street sweeper, a car park attendant, a nurse, a teacher, a bank clerk or a lawyer; simply decide to be thorough. Thoroughly great, thoroughly decent, thoroughly reliable, thoroughly researched, thoroughly briefed, thoroughly trained: simply be thorough. If you do, I guarantee that you and your circumstances will grow. You cannot fail to grow above your peers because most of them are not being thorough.

My Gran always said, "Leave a place better than you found it!" In other words, however you find something or anything, upgrade it! If it's the kitchen, leave it tidier; if it's a business, make sure it's more profitable; and if it's a friend, leave them wiser and feeling more loved than before. The attention to detail is what makes the difference. Thoroughness in your craft – whatever that craft is – will set you above the people who just want to get by. Learn to be thorough. It will cost you in time and effort, but you will be rewarded – whether it be in your promotion, profit, self-fulfilment or all of them, you will prosper.

The modern world will push you for quantity; it will ask you to cut corners and let go of your values. It is a trap. Learn the truth that quality and thoroughness will give better rewards in the long term. People will wait for a complete job; they will accept a delay if it means quality and they will pay more and return for a methodical service. In fact, the best companies only accept business that permits thoroughness. Any order that you accept where you cannot give it your best will eventually cost you more. Products manufactured without thoroughness need repairing and replacing much quicker.

A company or an individual which is thorough is destined for success. Look at the great works of art, the greatest of films and books: they all stand the test of time because their creators were conscientious in their thoroughness. Those who are thorough, grow. You will grow if you are motivated, because you show you care and respect for what you are doing or making.

… GROWTH THROUGH THOROUGHNESS

If you decide to become a master of your craft, then the attention to the smallest detail will become vital to you. If you were to go into hospital for an operation, would you like the surgeon to be thorough? If you were to go on an aeroplane, would you like the pilot to be thorough? If you were to go on a cruise, would you like the captain to be thorough as he guides the ship through difficult waters? We all want a thorough dentist, a thorough mechanic, a thorough chef, but often we won't be thorough ourselves.

Thoroughness will take you above and beyond most of your peers. Growth will happen if you decide to pay attention to what most people overlook. When you study successful stories, you will find that those who succeeded had a spirit of excellence. Someone once said, "All that is needed is an ounce of knowledge, an ounce of intelligence and a pound of thoroughness."

Often it is the anticipation of tomorrow or what is up ahead that compromises our attention to the smallest detail. However, if we will put the big picture to one side for a while, concentrate on where we are and commit ourselves to the job at hand, we will grow. If we do our best with the gifts, abilities and skills given to us today, then tomorrow's successes will take care of themselves.

The satisfaction gained by doing your best is beyond measure. Whatever you create is judged by its usefulness and beauty rather than how long it took to complete it. So, embrace today and the moment you are in. Decide to commit to it. Don't yearn for tomorrow and cut corners to get there; thoroughness will not just get you to your destination, but it will give you joy on the journey. Make it a habit. Habits come by committing daily to the same task again and again. You can achieve it; you just need to practice repeatedly.

Contentment comes from being thorough in the smallest details. Be thorough as a husband, a wife, a boss, a pastor, an employee or whatever role you find yourself in. Frustration comes in a relationship when one is thorough and the other couldn't care less. God has been detailed with your creation and your conversion. Nothing has been left to chance. He wants you to grow. Don't frustrate Him and His plans by your refusal to commit thoroughly. If you do that, then you and your future possibilities won't grow. If you do commit and engage in the smallest details, then all things become possible. Check your weaknesses, and if you have a lack of discipline in an area, then commit yourself to being meticulous and just wait to see what will happen in your future. Whatever your work is, do it seriously and extensively and never leave it half done. Most people look for short cuts, but there is no short cut to being rigorously thorough.

Decide to be thorough each day. Attack each day vigorously. Give it your very best and exhaust every opportunity and chance to serve that you have. Life will reward you when you consistently give your very best. Most people don't, so you will automatically be ahead of the game. Rewards will come and so will opportunities. People pay more, and due respect is given when they perceive someone is going the extra mile for them. We pay average wages for average; we pay more for excellence. Who wants to go to an average restaurant, receive average service and have an average time? We will pay more for excellence. There is nothing more frustrating than eating at a fine restaurant and receiving average service. The food and the surroundings are amazing, yet the attention is poor. The waiter or waitress is not interested in you. They are not mindful of you or careful with their service. People pick up a lack of sincerity; when someone is superficial, it is apparent.

If you decide to give less than 100%, it will continue to cost you. It will cost you financially as well as relationally. People know when you have stopped trying. When you have stopped giving your best. The work rate decreases, the attitude diminishes, the targets aren't met. Some people think they are getting away with it – and maybe they are, for a while. Reality tells us that it catches up on you. Relationships fall into disrepair. Employers begin to make other arrangements. Bank balances may even fall. Opportunities dry up. Eventually, there is a price to pay for the lack of commitment that you have shown. Motivation must be sought every day. Look for people and situations that will encourage you to give your very best. Please don't wait for your boss to motivate you. Some never will. They may just sack you or put you out to pasture and decide you are simply not worth bothering with. An employer or a customer sits up and takes notice when they have an employee or supplier who is going the extra mile.

As a Pastor, I have noticed that the thoroughness someone applies to their home life and their work life is mostly the same thoroughness they apply to their relationship with God. If they are intentional at work, they will be intentional at home. If they are intentional at home, then that will be displayed in their faith. If they are half hearted at work, then that's the attitude elsewhere. Whatever your assignment and tasks are in life, attack them vigorously and with energy – it will bring the best out of you and of others.

Actions to help you GROW through THOROUGHNESS

1 Look at your work. Do you do just enough or more than enough? Why is that the case?

2 Where in your life could you benefit by being more thorough?

3 What are you going to do to make a start in that area?

4 When will you start?

5 Dedicate your life to be a master in your craft, not just an amateur of all sorts.

YOUR PATHWAY TO GROWTH

> ## Quotes on Thoroughness

"Accept business only at a price permitting thoroughness. Then do a thorough job, regardless of the cost."

- Arthur C. Nelson -

"Be thorough in all you do; and remember that although ignorance often may be innocent, pretension is always despicable."

- William E. Gladstone -

"People forget how fast you did a job; but they remember how well you did it."

- Howard W. Newton -

GROWTH THROUGH THOROUGHNESS

"Whatever is worth doing at all is worth doing well."

- Lord Chesterfield -

"When you can do the common things of life in an uncommon way, you will command the attention of the world."

- George Washington Carver -

"Every job is a portrait of the person who did it. Autograph your work with excellence."

- Abraham Lincoln -

CHAPTER TEN

10

GROWTH FOR TODAY

YESTERDAY IS HISTORY

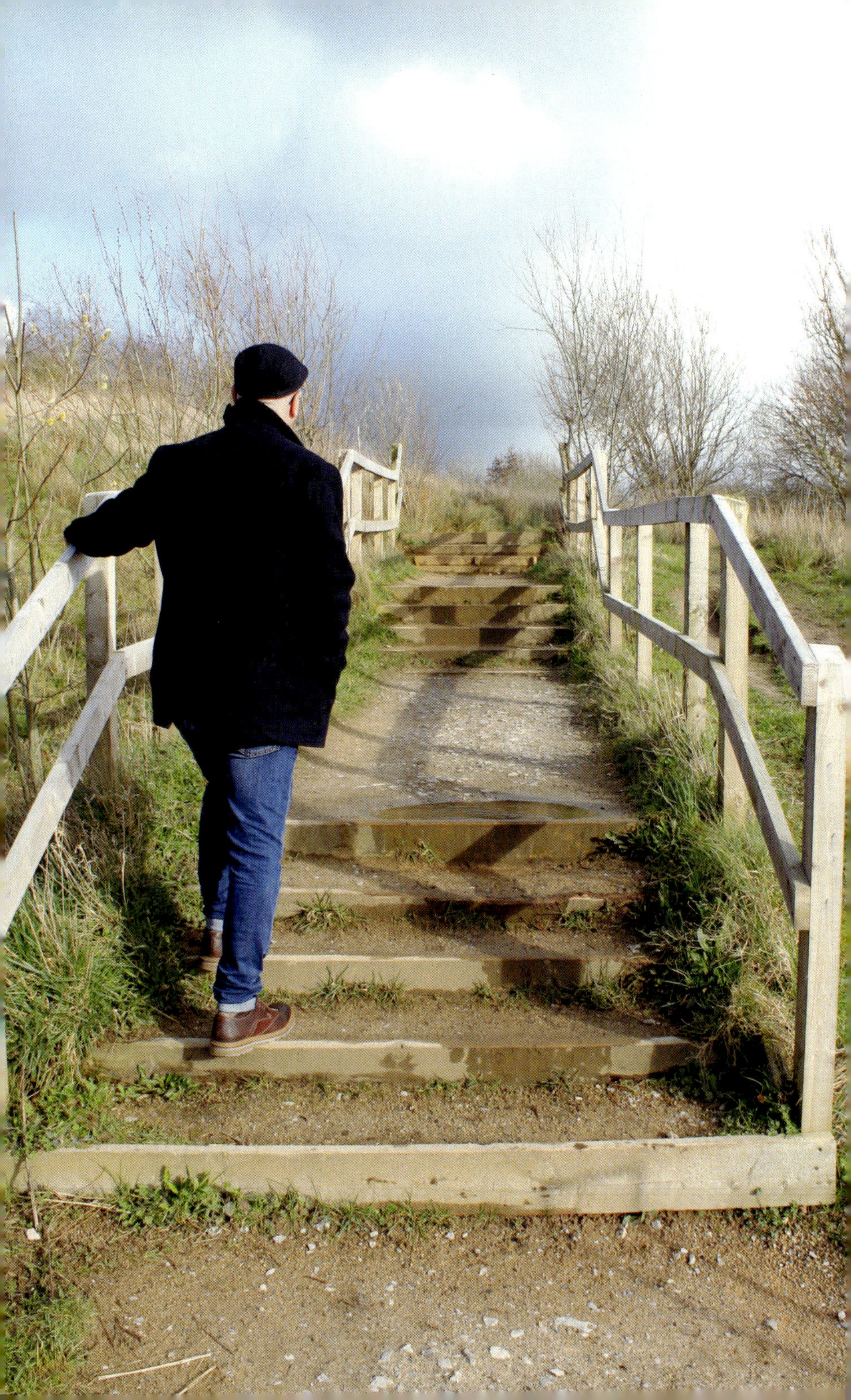

YOUR PATHWAY TO GROWTH

GROWTH FOR TODAY

People dream that today will be the day everything changes for the better; they long for it to be the turning point in their lives. Yet the truth is, we will reap today what we sowed yesterday. If we live correctly today, then we will grow tomorrow; today is vital for tomorrow's success.

Today is the only day you must deal with. It will reveal to you what your real values have been. You can talk well, but can you live well? Today will bring blessings and challenges, but you must decide you will grow because of experiencing today. Most people waste today; they spend too much time longing for tomorrow, not realising that tomorrow will just repeat the emptiness and despondency they feel today. The best preparation for tomorrow is today. If you want your tomorrow to be different, then you need to start a new routine by valuing the day you have and choosing what will fill your today. Yesterday is gone and tomorrow has not yet come; today is the day, so use it well.

Have you ever heard the saying, "Yesterday is history, tomorrow is a mystery, but today is a gift – that's why it's called the present?" Be thankful for the 24 hours you have been given. You have 86,400 seconds to be grateful for. True gratitude comes through the decision to use this precious time wisely.

GROWTH FOR TODAY

Look at your plans for today, if indeed you have any. Some people pack their days with plans and some people wait and see what happens. If you are going to grow, you need to plan your day and maximise the 24 hours you have been given. Today is a gift. You don't need to make the same mistakes as yesterday – undo your bad habits and create good ones.

Do you have a list to achieve today? If you will face the problem, the pain and the difficulty of today, it will make it easier to deal with tomorrow. Procrastination is many people's biggest enemy; they don't want to face today in hope it will disappear overnight, but that just makes it worse. If you continually put off the trials of life, you will find that the motivation for today slowly disappears. If you will discipline yourself today, you will enjoy the fruits of tomorrow. John Maxwell puts it this way:

"We exaggerate yesterday. We overestimate tomorrow. We underestimate today."

Every today is the most important day of your life. Your vision for tomorrow will be incubated today. Today might be dark and you might be lonely, but all life starts in a dark place. The seed put in the ground today will one day be the flower, the bush or the tree. Every time you walk through the forest, look at the trees and bushes and realise they all started with a seed. The baby in the darkness of the womb today will be new born tomorrow, all because of a seed.

Plant the seeds today for your tomorrow. Invest today and reap the harvest tomorrow. Begin a great new habit today. Decide to stop a bad habit at the same time. According to University College London, it takes 66 days to create a new habit; if you begin today you only have 65 to go. A bad habit doesn't go away by itself – it needs your help. Habits decide your future, not a wish list. Today is a fantastic opportunity to seize the day and embrace the growth you intend for tomorrow.

The danger comes when we spend our tomorrows today. Tomorrow's money, earnings and gifts; when we borrow, we reap where we haven't sown. Today is the day to invest so that you have something tomorrow. Don't sell your today cheaply. When you have employment, you are selling your today for a financial reward. You are valuable and your task is to make yourself even more valuable. People pay great money for value. The future belongs to those who prepare for it now. The great thing about tomorrow is that it comes one day at a time. Don't be

YOUR PATHWAY TO GROWTH

overwhelmed about tomorrow; you only need to face today. An acorn today will one day be an oak tree.

I have concluded that one of the main reasons people fail to grow is their own low self-esteem. They haven't invested each day in themselves. They may have looked after the kids and been the best mother and father they could be. They try and keep fit and have medicals regularly, but they fail to look after how they perceive themselves. Subsequently, they often feel negative about themselves. They put on a smile, they laugh, they play the game of life, but all along they are feeling defeated by their low self-esteem. If you are a Christian, you cannot allow this to continue. Every day, you need to feed yourself. Feed yourself the truth, and not the lies that have been planted in your yesterdays. Today is the day to change what has been sown so that you can change what you are going to reap tomorrow. As a Christian, you can use these truths to declare your reality:

John 1:12 - *I am a child of God!*

John 15: 1 -15 - *I am a branch of the true vine, and a conduit of Christ's life.*

John 15:15 - *I am a friend of Jesus.*

Romans 3:24 - *I have been justified and redeemed.*

Romans 6:6 - *My old self was crucified with Christ.*

Romans 8:1 - *I will not be condemned by God.*

Romans 8:2 - *I have been set free from the law of sin and death.*

Romans 8:17 - *As a child of God, I am a fellow heir with Christ.*

Romans 15:7 - *I have been accepted by Christ.*

1 Corinthians 1:2 - *I have been called a saint*

1 Corinthians 1:30 - *In Christ, I have wisdom, righteousness, sanctification and redemption.*

1 Corinthians 6:19 - *My body is the temple of the Holy Spirit who dwells in me.*

1 Corinthians 6:17 - *I am joined to the Lord and one in spirit with Him.*

2 Corinthians 2:14 - *God leads me in the triumph and knowledge of Christ.*

2 Corinthians 3:14 - *The hardening of my mind has been removed in Christ.*

2 Corinthians 5:17 - *I am a new creature in Christ.*

Galatians 5:1 - *I have been set free in Christ.*

Ephesians 1:3 - *I have been blessed with every spiritual blessing in the heavenly places.*

Ephesians 1:4 - *I am chosen, holy and blameless before God.*

Ephesians 2:10 - *I am God's workmanship created to produce good works.*

Ephesians 5:8 - *I was formerly darkness, but now I am light in the Lord.*

Philippians 4:19 - *God supplies all my needs.*

1 Thessalonians 1:4 - *God loves me and has chosen me.*

Repeating these truths as a Christian every morning will boost your self-esteem. As you sow these God truths and you fertilise them with belief, they will take root and begin to change what's possible in your life. Zig Ziglar claimed, "It's impossible to consistently believe in a manner inconsistent with how we see ourselves. We can do very few things in a positive way if we feel negative about ourselves."

Today, you can start to grow by beginning to change how you perceive yourself. Start to value who you are and what you are. You are more than what you currently perceive.

If you are not a Christian, then the good news of Jesus is that you can be. If you are a Christian but haven't been taking your faith seriously, then decide from this moment. Today can be the day that you decide to grow in your faith.

Today is vital. You have such potential, but perhaps you have not been appreciative of what God has given you. Perhaps you have not been managing your possibilities well, so you haven't grown. Today and every other day, that can change. My friend, it's time to grow. Today truly is your day of salvation. Make today count.

YOUR PATHWAY TO GROWTH

Here are some practical ingredients to make today count in your growth cycle. These are what I endeavour to do. It doesn't always work out every day, but these are my goals in no particular order:

- Personal devotions
- Personal development and training
- Personal exercise
- Coffee - a great detoxifier
- Encourage and invest in someone
- Read and write
- Listen to people, to God, to podcasts, to audio books
- Relax
- Meditate
- Give something away
- Spend time in your home.

There are many more ingredients to a healthy today.

A great day has certain ingredients. Become responsible for what goes into your day. Try fasting from being negative about yourself for a day and feed yourself with positive scriptures. You will sow great seeds and tomorrow you will have a prosperous harvest. Speak to the mountains in your life and see them disappear. You don't need to climb the mountains; you just need to speak to them and see them dissolve. Speak to the mountain of insecurity, inferiority, insolvency, illness, illiteracy, illegality, illegitimacy and any other ills in your life. Speak truth every day to these negatives and see them crumble.

A great day needs composing just like a symphony does. If you tell me that prayer, the Bible, your family, your church, your hobbies and your health are important, but you don't act today and cherish these vital parts of your life, then how can anyone believe you? An occasional bunch of flowers, a random visit to the doctors, a yearly visit to church, a short weekly walk – these things don't match up today to what you planned so confidently yesterday. Today is a brilliant opportunity to start again and let your words and actions match up.

.... **GROWTH FOR TODAY**

At the end of your life, I guarantee you will ask, "Where have all the years gone?" The truth is, those years have disappeared day by day. The day you are living in today is to be treasured and spent wisely. In this chapter, I have tried to help you see the value of today, and to see the wisdom in deciding to grow today so that one day in the future you won't be looking back in disappointment – rather, you will look back through the years and see just how far you have travelled.

Actions to help you GROW through TODAY

1 On a scale of 1-10 what number would you give to your value of today?

2 What investment have you made in yourself today? What dividends have you seen today from previous investments made in days past?

3 Do you have a 'To do' list each day?

4 Do you prepare each day for the next day? How do you do that?

5 Change your daily habits. Decide to adopt good habits and drop the bad ones. Decide to be proactive and intentional.

❝ Today quotes

"What you know today can affect what you do tomorrow. But what you know today cannot affect what you did yesterday."

- Condoleezza Rice -

"The future starts today, not tomorrow."

- Pope John Paul 11 -

"The best preparation for tomorrow is to do today's work superbly well."

- William Osler -

"One today is worth two tomorrows."

- Benjamin Franklin -

"Today is a most unusual day, because we have never lived it before; we will never live it again; it is the only day we have."

- Willian A Ward -

CHAPTER ELEVEN

11

GROWTH BEYOND YOUR TRADITION

YOUR FUTURE DEMANDS IT

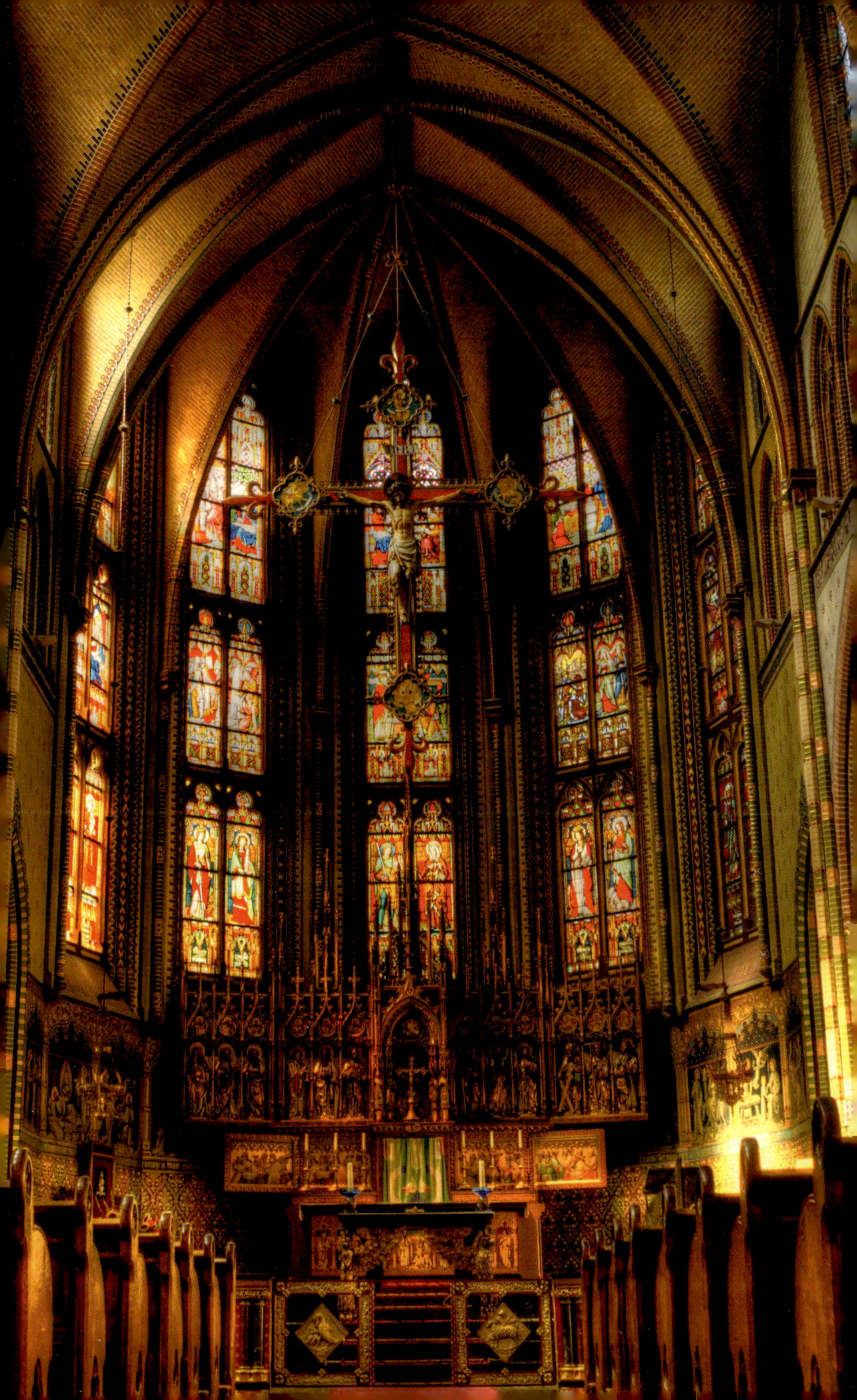

GROWTH BEYOND YOUR TRADITION

Many people reject their tradition. I find that regrettable. They reject the way they were raised and the values they were brought up with, whether it be in a religious, societal or familial sense.

They feel they have grown out of it and it has nothing further to offer. Sometimes tradition can be viewed as something that once gained new ground: it was radical in its day, yet over time it has become outdated and the passion and the purpose has gone out of it. I don't think tradition should be rejected; instead, it should be used as a platform to grow into new ground. In fact, what it was originally can become even more radical and more productive than it was before. I think Jesus is a perfect example of this. He was bringing freedom and life to old religion, yet it was his habit – his tradition – to go to the temple each week on the Sabbath. He rejected the Pharisees' hypocrisy, but he didn't reject their basic tradition of gathering together to worship God.

We visit many churches as we travel around the world and we have had the privilege of experiencing many different traditions and cultures. Some of them have certain ways of operating, but they are not always rooted in scripture. Let me give you some illustrations. When I was young, I was raised in a tradition that I am thankful to God for, even though it was legalistic. I remember the time when some young married couples were wanting to organise a barbecue, so they printed some posters on dayglo paper to promote the event. I overheard my mother having a conversation with a friend complaining about the barbecue. My mother was trying to appease her friend whose husband was in leadership of the church, by telling her the barbecue was just a picnic. I was only a young boy, but I remember thinking it was funny when the friend said, "If it's just a picnic, why can't they just call it a picnic?" The custom and tradition of the church at that time suggested the word 'barbecue' was in someway lawless and wrong, but the word 'picnic' was right. This is the tradition and set of values I was part of. Nevertheless, it was full of people who loved Jesus, the movement was radical, and there was tremendous growth and freedom in its earlier days. Yet the time came when it stopped growing; certain values were becoming outdated. It was becoming a tradition.

This illustration might sound ridiculous and from another world, and in some ways it is, but I wonder what tradition you will fight people on that has long since lost its true meaning.

Growth needs to go beyond traditional add-ons. Ask yourself: in your tradition, what baggage has been given to you to carry? If it is precious, life giving, freedom enabling, biblical and full of grace, keep it. However, if it's man-made and full of no real purpose, then question it and decide whether you need to continue to carry that dead weight. Remember, we are talking about growth and you cannot grow in a straitjacket. There should always be room to grow and develop. If you are in a situation where you cannot go forward and mature, ask yourself and your leaders why? You might not like the answers, but it helps you go forward, whatever they say. If they are simply blocking you for no good reason, then it's time to move on because you are not going to grow in that soil. If there is a good reason, whether you like it or not, it's an opportunity to change. Ask what you can and should do. What training needs to happen? What do you need to apply yourself to?

There have been many reasons why people have left our congregation. I remember one person saying that they couldn't stay in our church because we didn't pray for an hour in tongues before the service. I remember another person saying we were too casual. One person wanted to leave because we mentioned money too much, yet another person complained because they thought we didn't mention money enough. Yet another complained because my wife is a pastor.

YOUR PATHWAY TO **GROWTH**

In leadership we have learned that some people are more concerned about having things the way they have always been, rather than being willing to grow personally and corporately. They prefer the security of tradition, rather than the risk of new adventures. We hate change, don't we? Change the seats in church and people ask why. Change the format and people leave. Change where you meet and there is sometimes mutiny. Yet when you don't change, people grumble too. Sometimes people are so stuck that when they finally decide to change, they don't just change a few things – they change everything. That's our humanity. Sometimes it's all or nothing. Gain new ground by constantly moving forward gradually. This book is a great example. I never sat down and just wrote it. I had to write it slowly and deliberately. I analysed my work. I asked others to examine it too. I gave them the right to speak into my work. Sometimes I left it alone for a few days and then came back to it with a new vigour. Flexibility is key. Don't get bogged down in your life; keep things fresh.

It's only when you begin to analyse and question the traditions that we have that you give yourself permission to grow. I want to give you permission to question what's important to you and why that is. If it's Godly and biblical, don't ditch it. However, if it is man-made tradition then let man have it and you choose to develop!

Whether your traditions and values are cultural or religious, be sure of this: always look out for new ground and take it – your future demands it. I sometimes wonder what the New Testament apostles would make of the 21st Century Church. What would John and Charles Wesley make of the Methodist church that operates near you? What would the founding fathers think of the Brethren movement that I grew up in and the barbecue or picnic dispute and the dayglo paper? What would John the Baptist think of the Baptist Union.

As current leaders, my question is, "Are we as radical as our spiritual forefathers?" Often, we seem to be more radical in self-serving, empire building, stretching and bending truth till it breaks, rather than trying to emulate great men and women of God who blazed a trail for God and saw the tremendous growth that we dream about, personally and corporately.

Ruth in the Bible is someone who grew beyond her tradition. Ruth's mother-in-law was moving away. She tried to persuade Ruth and Orpah, her daughters-in-law, to stay behind (Ruth 1). Ruth, however, had a different plan. She wanted to go forward into a new situation; she wanted to leave her past behind and grow into her possibilities. She told Naomi, "Your people will be my people and your God shall be my God." (Ruth 1:16)

Ruth powerfully confessed and declared her future. She was willing to grow beyond her tradition. I wonder if you are? Yes, it's scary, threatening and it's a clean break from your past, but if you are willing to put your past behind you and grow towards your future, you can change your destiny. Tradition can be a wonderful friend, yet, on the other hand, it can be an inhibiting enemy. Put it to one side and grab your future. The Bible says, in Matthew 11:12, 'the Kingdom of heaven suffers violence, and the violent take it by force.' In other words, take what's rightfully yours. No one will offer or cajole you into taking it; you must grasp it. It's your life and you are ultimately responsible for it. Tradition is your guidance, so learn from it, but don't serve it as an idol.

Remember, the people who formed the tradition didn't want you to worship the tradition – they wanted you to worship the God they worshipped and had fallen in love with. The tradition was a means to an end, so don't fall in love with their tradition. It was a vehicle they used to get nearer to the God they trusted. They wanted you to have the passion, the purpose, the presence that they enjoyed. If you do that, you will grow above and beyond all you could ever ask or think. In other words, hold your tradition close if you so desire, but hold God closer. They wanted you to take the baton they were passing you and run your race. Rather than run around in circles doing laps of the tradition, they desired that you would go further, go faster and take off from the runway they had conscientiously built. I believe they literally look over from Heaven, as Hebrews chapter 12 tells us of a 'cloud of witnesses' watching to see just how far we can go. Anything that hinders your race, shake it off. God deserves and demands that, and you should too.

As I finish this chapter, may I say that certain traditions in our lives are certainly worth keeping and passing down. They give and keep shared values and keep the bond we have with those close to us. They reinforce the attachment we have with those who are important to us. They can be the glue that keeps us together. They create shared memories that create unity with those we love. So, I would encourage you to have traditions, even if your tradition is to have no tradition.

YOUR PATHWAY TO GROWTH

I have noticed that some sportsmen and women have certain rituals that they keep strictly to when they are taking part in their sport. They may raise their hands to the sky, they may cross themselves, tie their laces – even though they don't need to be tied – or adjust their shirt, socks or hair. They have certain procedures and traditions they feel they must go through, and if they don't, then their momentum and confidence is affected. It's reported that Michael Jordan, the famous basketball player, wore North Carolina shorts below his Chicago Bulls shorts out of some sort of tradition. According to Argosy University, this sort of tradition brings self-confidence to a player. It doesn't change their talent, but it builds confidence because of the routine.

Actions to help you GROW through your TRADITION

1 What traditions in your childhood are you still thankful for? Why?

2 Name something that you do as a tradition that no longer serves any purpose. Drop it today.

3 Evaluate how you worship God. Is it just a tradition, or could it be transformed into something more authentic?

4 Start a new tradition – a life-giving habit.

5 Ask those around you what traditions they enjoy and why?

Quotes on Tradition

"See to it that no one takes you captive by philosophy and empty deceit, according to human tradition, according to the elemental spirits of the world, and not according to Christ."

- Colossians 2:8 ESV -

"Many people feel so pressured by the expectations of others that it causes them to be frustrated, miserable and confused about what they should do. But there is a way to live a simple, joy-filled, peaceful life, and the key is learning how to be led by the Holy Spirit, not the traditions or expectations of man."

- Joyce Meyer -

"Thus you nullify the Word of God by your tradition that you have handed down. And you do many things like that."

- Mark 7 v 13 -

"The less there is to justify a traditional custom, the harder it is to get rid of it."

- Mark Twain (The Adventures of Tom Sawyer) -

CHAPTER TWELVE

12

GROWTH THROUGH TRAVEL

TO TRAVEL IS TO LIVE!

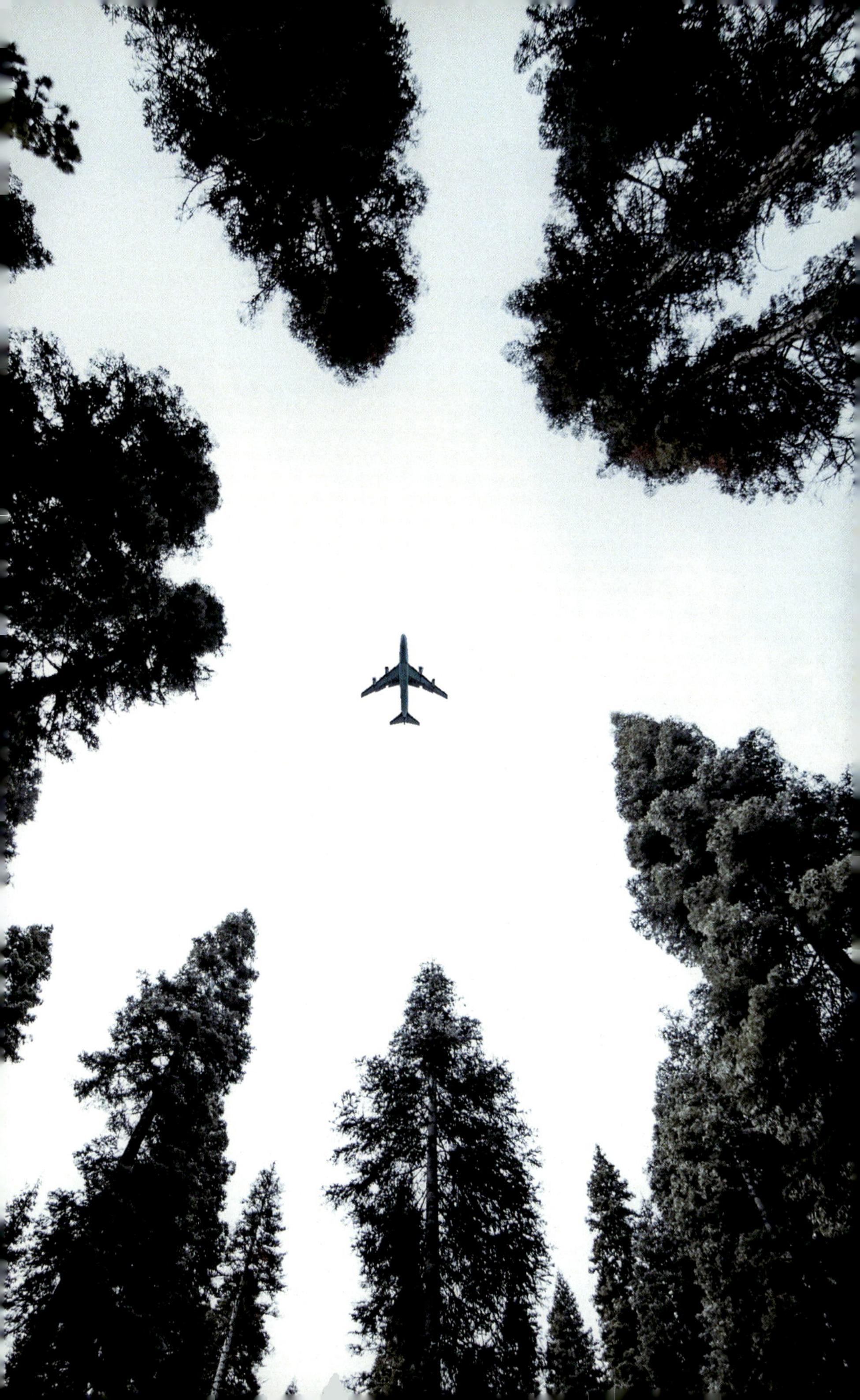

YOUR PATHWAY TO GROWTH

GROWTH THROUGH TRAVEL

There is a lot to learn through travelling, and often it's not the destination but the journey itself that matters. It's the people we meet, the places we see and the cultural differences that inspire and give us new insight into God's world.

We often travel by plane and the difference between a good flight and a great flight is amazing. I remember when we were travelling to the USA and I asked, in my usual cheeky Scottish way, if there was any chance of an upgrade. For the first time, the attendant took me seriously and she looked at her computer. She stared at it for a while and then she called her colleague to look at it. She then called her supervisor to have another look and this got my attention. I asked what was so interesting and she announced to me that we could be upgraded to first class from economy for £40 each! Our travel suddenly became a different story. Fillet steak was the order of the day; lying flat out and sleeping over the Atlantic was a new experience. We arrived at our destination refreshed and blessed. That day there was a whole new experience to be had, only a few seats further up the very same plane we often travelled on.

You too can grow by travelling. Every year, we travel to the USA to attend conferences and to preach. We love going but we rarely enjoy the journey – in fact, sometimes we dread it because the jet lag is testing. To be clear, we don't often fly first class, but life is not always about the destination; it's more often about the journey.

I have found that God gives us a vision or a dream, and then He takes us back to the beginning of the journey. He announces to us over the tannoy in our spirits that He will go with us on the journey towards the dream. The 40 years in the wilderness for the Israelites was not to get them out of Egypt, but to get Egypt out of them. They weren't ready for the promised land. The travelling should only have taken days, but it took 40 years for them to be ready. How long will your journey last? Decide you will grow quickly. Learn fast. Travel first class and arrive – not half dead but refreshed.

As I was travelling from New Delhi to London, I looked around the flight to see all sorts of people on their travels. Some were bored, some sleeping, while others were watching various films and programmes. In the 7-and-a-half-hour flight, I had written thousands of words. The journey went quickly, and it had been productive.

Many of us are just passing time, waiting and hoping for the good times to arrive. The journey becomes irrelevant, but that's not how it's meant to be. You are supposed to enjoy the journey and it's meant to be productive. Your journey is meant to be helpful to others. If you decide to grow in this area, you will stop acting like the child in the back of the car asking, "Are we there yet?" and you will start appreciating the scenery around you. Decide you are going to travel with style and class, wherever you are seated on the plane of life.

It's a bit like the day you were born: the start of your journey through life. The sun came up and your years began. You began to adapt and learn new skills. Your parents trained and educated you, and your feet began to take you on your own personal journey. Your mind began to expand, and your gifting and skills opened doors for you.

Travelling began – not just for a gap year, but through your life. Are you travelling well and enjoying the journey? You will go through different seasons and some will be hard and frosty, while others will be warm and sunny. Are you travelling easy? Or is life hitting you hard and knocking you back? Are you receding into a cocoon of self-preservation, or are you travelling with an expansive mindset?

YOUR PATHWAY TO **GROWTH**

Has the sun gone down early for you? Have you pulled up the drawbridge of your life and decided the travelling is not worth it? If so, the devil is lying to you. It doesn't have to be that way. The journey is meant to be enjoyable and not just endured. God wants you to do life differently by deciding that every season and every pathway has a plan just for you.

Often on our journeys, we have been so focussed on our pasts that we have failed to open our eyes to see what God wants to reveal to us. It's almost as if we would rather watch fake life than see real life. Growth on your travels is seen when you start to see what you need is to become all that you were meant to be. The more well-travelled you are, the bigger the opportunity you have had to grow. People around the world have so much to teach us. My wife Sue and I have friends in many nations. We are indebted to them for the lessons they have taught us. Robert Louis Stevenson said; "For my part, I travel not to go anywhere, but to go. I travel for travel's sake. The great affair is to move."

"Travel teaches toleration," according to Benjamin Disraeli. It teaches you why people behave the way they do. Saint Augustin put it this way: "The World is a book, and those who do not travel read only a page."

I want to encourage you to travel. If you cannot afford to at this moment, then begin to plan and dream about it. Write down where you would like to go. When Sue was a little girl, she dreamt of travelling to various nations. In the last few years, we have travelled to those precise places. She had the vision to go and God knew the timing. Travel in your mind and spirit, and your body will catch up one day. Never let finance kill your dream. Money always follows vision. If you have the vision and the dream to travel, the finance will fall into place. You may have to sacrifice and save, but it will come about.

Travelling enlarges you. It helps you grow to a level you couldn't at home. It teaches you independence and how to communicate in different cultures. It teaches you about different people groups and it will change your perspective. If you are from the West, you will normally see how rich you are compared to most of the world. This should humble you and make you realise the futility of riches. You come back with a new appreciation for what you took for granted previously.

....GROWTH THROUGH TRAVEL

Journeys create memories, some of which will never be forgotten. Being out of your comfort zone enables you to grow. In fact, discomfort is often an indication of growth.

Actions to help you GROW through your TRAVEL

1 Growth is a journey. Are you committed to begin travelling to a better place?

2 How big is your world? Is your outlook shrinking or increasing? Do you think globally or locally? Why do you think that is?

3 Do you enjoy meeting people from other cultures, or are you naturally suspicious of them? Decide to go outside of your groupings and enjoy other cultures.

4 Book a trip further than you have been before. It's not how far that counts, just make it further than your last journey.

5 Read a missionary classic and see how a missionary like David Livingston or Hudson Taylor changed nations through travel.

> Quotes on Travel

"The Christian experience from start to finish, is a journey of faith."

- Watchman Nee -

"Life is either a daring adventure, or nothing."

- Helen Keller -

"To travel is to live!"

- Hans Christian Anderson -

"Christ likeness is your eventual destination, but your journey will last a lifetime."

- Rick Warren -

"Go everywhere in the world and tell the good news to everyone."

- Mark 16 v 15 -

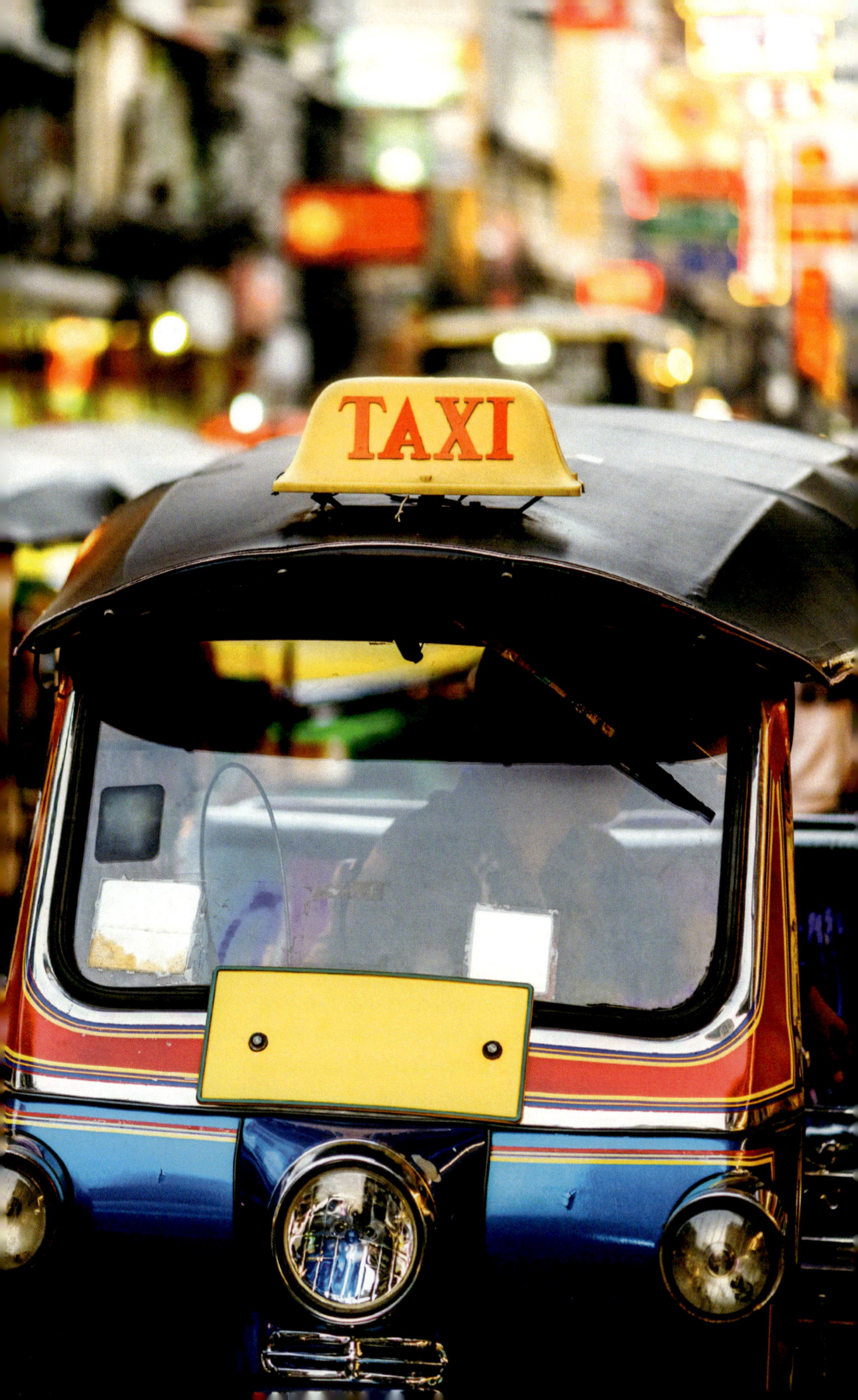
TAXI

CHAPTER THIRTEEN

13

GROWTH THROUGH TIME

GROWTH TAKES TIME

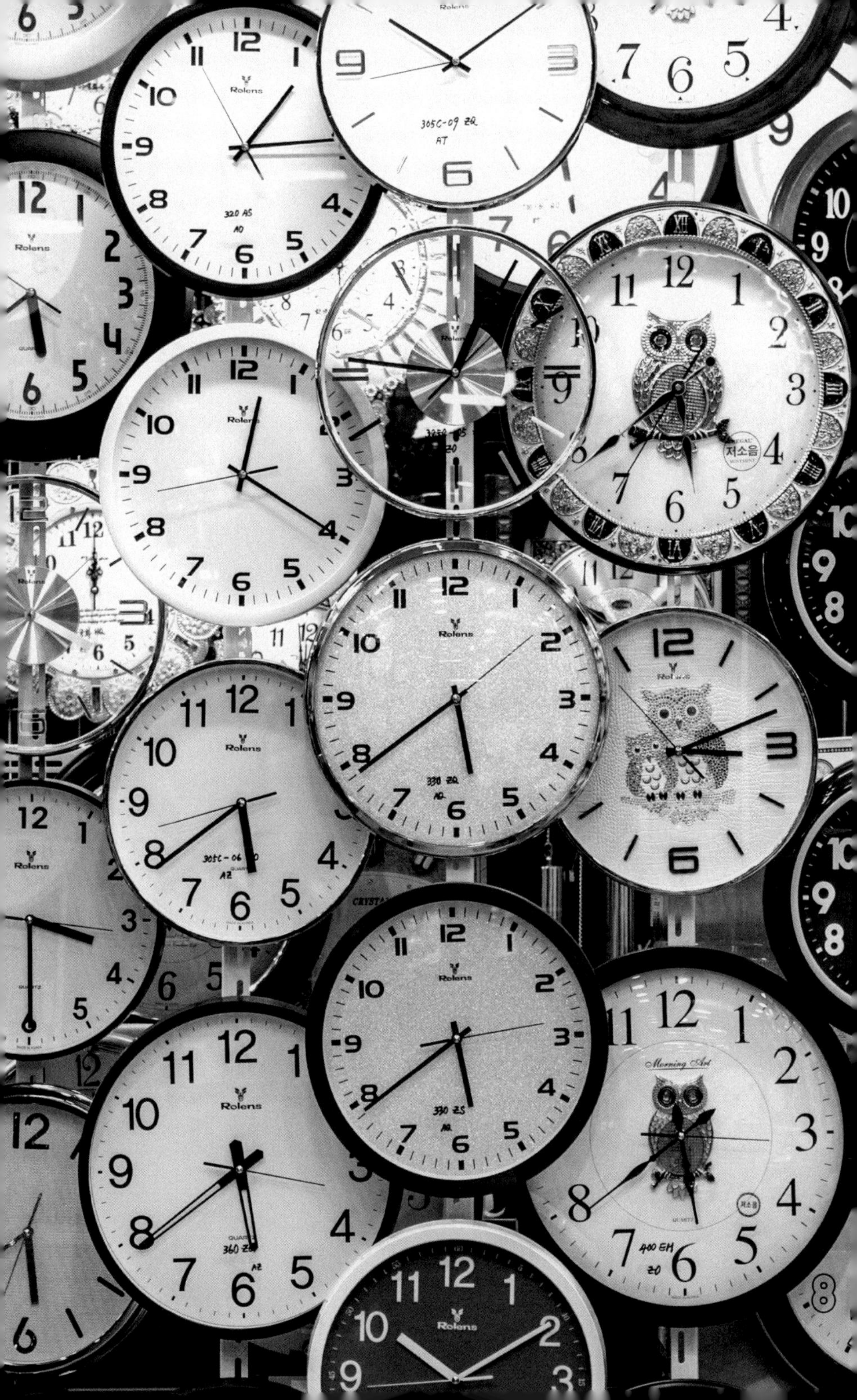
Rolens
305C-09 ZQ
AT
320 AS
저소음
330 ZQ
Morning Art
330 ZS

YOUR PATHWAY TO **GROWTH**

GROWTH THROUGH TIME

Growth takes time. Therein lies what most people believe is the problem, in relation to personal growth. Time is a much sought-after component for the busy person. How is it a person can rule a nation, be a president or run a multinational company in the same time we struggle to run our comparatively simple lives? We complain that we don't have enough of it. We use it as a reason for not achieving more. We yearn for more time off, more down time and extra leisure time. We talk about having quality time with someone we live with. Time, they say, waits for no man. It rolls along relentlessly at 60 seconds per minute, 60 minutes per hour, 24 hours per day and 7 days per week. We usually have 52 weeks in a year and, before you know it, the days of your childhood are over, and you are married with children of your own. Middle age approaches and responsibilities eat up your schedule. Where has all the time gone?

The Bible tells us to redeem it. Have you ever considered how much you waste? It's far too valuable and limited as a resource to let it drift. It's more precious than gold. In fact, with employment we trade time for money. Never stay in a job wasting time just doing something for money. Your time is too valuable. Use your time doing something that brings value to you and to others. Your days are numbered, so be aware of that fact and treasure the time allocated to you.

GROWTH THROUGH TIME

I want to look at maximising your time so that you are productive in all you seek to do. Achieving greatness in your life will mean measuring and allocating your time carefully. Doing just what you feel like doing all the time cannot be tolerated. I never felt like starting this book. I didn't feel like getting out of bed this morning. In most cases, you must get on with it and do right before you feel right.

I hear people say I need more time, but there is no more time being manufactured for you. There is no more time to be given; it just needs to be managed better. There will only ever be 365 days available to you, so we must become better at managing the time we are given.

Evaluate your last twenty-four hours. Think back to how long you slept. Sleep is important, but how much do you need? One hour less sleep per night gives you an extra fifteen twenty-four-hour days per year in time to invest in yourself. In fifty years, that amounts to more than two years of time becoming available to you. That's just sleep.

Now, let's look at travel time. The average commute in the UK is two hours per day. Ten hours per week. This book was written while I have been travelling. I could have watched films or read magazines, but instead I used the time available to me productively. Many people have said to me, "I wish I had the time to write a book." The truth is, we all have the time.

How about your journey to and from work? Are you using that productively? Are you reading/listening to books or podcasts, or do you just look out of the window or argue with road users? Your time is too valuable to waste. There are only so many springs and summers in your life. If you don't plant in the spring and water in the summer of life, then you won't be able to reap in the autumn. Life is made up of seasons, and you only have so many.

Let's look at your leisure time. Many people just go brain dead in the evening. They plant themselves in front of a TV and go into zombie mode. A recent study by Reebok suggests we spend 41% of our lives looking at a technological device and just 0.69% exercising. Of course, we all need to relax, but what is the quality of your relaxation? Remember: rubbish in, rubbish out. Are you exercising at all? The same study said we spend nearly 30% of our life sitting down. Do you

YOUR PATHWAY TO GROWTH

meditate on God's word? Mediation, like exercise, reduces stress. It helps control anxiety and enhance self-awareness. Fill your mind with scripture and God thoughts. Take a scripture and meditate on it. Let it soak in and permeate your inner being.

How about your lunch hours? How do you spend them? Are they invested or frittered away? As I write this chapter, I am having lunch in a café as my wife does some shopping. Use the time you have available to the maximum. Furthermore, I read recently that in a lifetime we spend 1.5 years on the toilet, and men spend more time there than ladies! Do you see what I'm am trying to say? Use your time wisely. Are you beginning to see how much time most of us waste? Life is too short to mismanage your time. Time management is not just a trendy phrase; it's a lesson to be learned well.

Do you pray? I wonder if you realise that prayer gives you a longer life? A survey by the Journal of Gerontology found, after asking 4,000 senior citizens, that those who took the time to pray coped better with illness and lived longer. In fact, it was found by the Bowling Green State University that meditation and prayer helped reduce the number of headaches people experienced. They asked people to take 20 minutes of time each day to repeat a spiritual mantra such as, "God is good. God is peace. God is love." A second group were asked to repeat a non-spiritual mantra such as, "Grass is green, sand is soft." After a month, those who used the spiritual mantra had fewer headaches and greater pain tolerance than the non-spiritual mantra users. The non-spiritual senior citizens continued to have the same symptoms as before.

Do you give yourself enough time to read? Reading regularly improves your mind and your memory. It stimulates you mentally and increases your knowledge. It improves your vocabulary, your focus and your concentration. You become more analytical as you spend more time reading, and it reduces stress. Studies have shown that the brain experiences the same serenity when you read as you do while you are in meditation. You can travel the world sitting in your favourite armchair – no passport or money needed. No delayed flights and passport control or check in needed. The growth you can receive by reading is limitless.

My third question is, do you have the wisdom to say, "No"? One of the biggest time wasters can be saying 'yes' when you should be saying 'no'. Some people struggle to say 'no'. Usually, it's the high achievers who say 'no' because they are productive. They get things done so people come to them to make things happen. You waste everyone's time when you are not the best person for the job. Learn to say 'no'. People may struggle to accept your answer at first, but if handled courteously and an explanation is given, people may understand. You simply shouldn't do everything you are asked to do. Not because what you are being asked to do is wrong – it's just wrong for you.

My fourth question is, who are you spending time with? You are influenced by the average of the five people you spend most of your time with. Look around and see who are your five. Do you want to become like them? Is God one of your five? Why wouldn't you spend quality time with him? He knows best, loves best, inspires best, trains best and grows you best. Make sure He is one of your five. If you are married, make sure they are also one of the five. Having done that, who are the other three?

Do you take the time to recalibrate your mind and your schedule? Making small changes can make a huge difference in your life. The difference between winning and losing in life is often very small. Making these small changes continually will keep you ahead of the game. Successful people never look back and admire what they have achieved; they are always looking towards the next goal and making alterations to take it to the next level.

One day, Jesus' parents were looking for him. They thought he was just with the people of his age or relatives, but his answer is interesting: "Didn't you realise I must be about my Father's business?" (Luke 2:49). Jesus had an agenda. Do we have an agenda? Do we know what we are about? Are you filling your time wisely, or are you tossed about and following on with whatever other people are doing?

Growth comes from using the time you have been given wisely. Some people go to university and achieve a degree, whereas others just go to university. Both had exactly the same amount of time. 25% of students work in the area they took their degree, 75% work in a different field and more than 33% regret going to university in the first place. As you look back in your life, can you see wasted time?

YOUR PATHWAY TO **GROWTH**

The question is not what you are going to do with the time already gone. The question to all of us is, what are we going to do with the time we have today? Take one day at a time and decide that each day you have, you will spend it wisely. People generally take more care spending their money than they do their time. As the old phrase says, 'time is money,' so let's take it seriously. Your biggest investment in life is not with money – it's with time!

Unless you are proactive, nothing will change and grow. You must take responsibility for your time. When I waste time, it frustrates me. Perhaps it's because I have fewer years ahead of me than I have behind me. I will achieve the best results from the time I am going to invest. Achieve the maximum out of your days, whatever it is that you are doing. Even if it's relaxing, then make sure your relaxation is profitable. You don't have to be busy all the time but be productive. Invest time with your loved ones. They won't always be there. In fact, you won't always be around either. Learn to talk. Ask probing questions. Ask open ended questions that don't just get a 'yes' or a 'no'. So often we say, "How are you"? They say, "Fine," and we move on. Why not ask a question like, "What have you done today that made you happy?" That makes a person think. Compliment people. Encourage them and show them love. Take the time to do that. It may sound elementary, but believe me, most people don't do it. Perhaps you think no one compliments you: try complimenting others and see the compliments return. You need to grow, and growers encourage, motivate and set the tone. Write the text, the letter, the email and make the call to invest encouragement into others. This is time well spent and you will grow because of these actions.

Growing hurts sometimes and managing your time might feel uncomfortable to begin with. For example, not sleeping as much will hurt at first. Not being with everyone in the canteen at lunchtime discussing the latest drama on TV will hurt at first. It just takes time to go through the growing pains and come out of the poverty of wasted time into the richness of time well spent.

Productive people are highly efficient with their time. In fact, you may have heard the phrase, 'If you want something done, ask the busy person to do it.' The person who has little to do won't find the time. As you begin to take time management seriously, you learn to prioritise. This begins to help your time

....**GROWTH THROUGH TIME**

become more efficient. Plan your day and plan your week, because time is a limited resource, therefore it is precious to you. Don't let people waste your time; they will try and steal your time too, but don't let them. Kindly and assertively protect your time and, as a result, you will grow.

Actions to help you GROW through your TIME

1 How much time do you think you waste daily? What was your weekly screen usage report on your smart phone recently? Write down the areas where you could use your time more wisely.

2 What could you fill that time with that would benefit you?

3 Pick a person who has gone further than you on the road you want to travel on. Spend time with them, ask them questions and learn. Spend time preparing for that meeting.

4 Do you meditate and pray? If not, when will you start?

5 Prepare a time schedule to activate the above using the time you are going to save from question 1.

Quotes on Time

"Time is what we want most, but what we use worst!"

- William Penn -

"Time is money!"

- Benjamin Franklin -

"Change your 24 hours and you will change your life!"

- Eric Thomas -

"Time is the most precious gift because you only have a set amount of it!"

- Rick Warren -

"In the time of my favour I heard you, and in the day of salvation I helped you. I tell you, now is the time of God's favour, now is the day of salvation."

- 2 Corinthians 6:2 NIV -

CONCLUSION

As you progress on your journey of growth, you will feel like stopping or find yourself de-motivated. In these times, determine to keep going forward. Take little steps and don't be hard on yourself. It's not how quickly you arrive at your destination, it's making sure you reach it and what you have learned along the way. Sometimes the journey is more important than the destination.

Whatever has awakened in you during the time of reading this book, make sure you tend to it. You are far more valuable than you have ever realised. People may not have recognised it, but you are amazing and have huge potential. Start where you are and get on the road. Some people ask, where should I begin or where should I head? I say to them, just begin by doing one thing – anything.

Take responsibility and be the CEO of your company rather than the customer. In other words, you must take charge and take control of your life. Most people act as though they are the customer and wait for direction. However, the smart people realise that there is more that can be offered; they are not onlookers, instead they roll up their sleeves and begin to be intentional about their life by taking responsibility and control.

Therefore, identify your gift. What makes you unique? Study, read, train and

CONCLUSION

research it. Anything you don't feed starves, so feed your talent. A lady phoned our food bank the other day and told me she had left her husband and needed food urgently. She had nothing to feed her children. Her abusive husband told her she would be back because he would starve her of money and resources. I promised her we would provide food and told her we were committed to her independence and safety. I found out she was going to college and was applying herself to study. As soon as she told me that, I knew she would come through her situation. Feed your potential and your potential will provide for your future. Starve your potential and your future diminishes.

You will find that as you grow, some people will be attracted to you and others will fall away. Be on guard. People who are attracted to you can be positive and negative. There will be some that want to suck the life out of you, and there will be some who want to work with you and for you. Avoid the former and be grateful for the latter. The ones who fall away are usually threatened or demotivated. Be careful to take with you those who are meant for you. Always try and include your partner, your friends or family in your growth journey. Read, watch and listen together so you grow together. There is something wonderful and magical about people growing together.

Before you can change the world, you must change your world. So, determine that you will work, change and grow. When you begin to BE something more, you will DO something more. You will be more active and intentional. When you DO more you will HAVE more, whether that be better relationships, financial rewards, a promotion or fulfilled dreams. Furthermore, make sure when you HAVE more you GIVE more. Giving is the fun part, as the Bible says it's better to GIVE than to receive. Giving is the best investment you will ever make.

Jesus says in John 10:10, "I have come that you may have life and life to the full." Many Christians wonder what happened to the full life. They sort of just wait for it to happen. They listen to all sorts of irrelevant communication, like negative news on TV, negative music, and the negative chatter that clogs our minds and spirits daily. These are some of the thieves that Jesus says steal and destroy in the earlier part of the verse. The full verse says, "The thief comes only to steal and destroy; I have come that they may have life and have it to the full." (John 10:10 NIV). Don't give your focus and concentration to the problem that has impacted you negatively. Decide to focus on the positive life that Jesus has offered you. Let it fill you up every day, so you can BE more each day. The way

YOUR PATHWAY TO GROWTH..

ahead is to put aside the past, and in the present decide you will BE all that God wants you to BE.

If you are plagued constantly with negative thoughts and emotions, let me give you a practical way of destroying what's killing you. Take a piece of A4 paper and write down every negative thought that comes to your mind daily. Write every single one of them down. When you have done that, literally kiss the sheet and these emotions goodbye and shred the sheet of paper. As you see the paper being shredded, picture all your negativity being destroyed. After shredding, you cannot read it and it's gone. If you have no access to a shredder, then burn the paper and see your negativity go up in smoke. Now have a look at what Jesus says about you (see Chapter 10). Read the statements and say them out loud. Don't just say them – choose to believe them. Put your faith and trust in them. The Bible is true because God is truth. Jesus said, "I am the way, the truth and the life." (John 14:6 NKJV). If you want life – abundant life – then you must follow His ways and His truth. Jesus said this to Thomas, who hadn't a clue what was going on. He was asking Jesus where He was going and how they (the disciples) could find the way. That is still true for us. Most of us don't know where we are going in life, and we also don't know where He is going either.

Faith makes it possible to do greater works than Jesus did. He said to the disciples and to us that we can do greater works. (John 14:12 NKJV). "Whatever you ask, that I will do, that the Father may be glorified in the Son. If you ask anything in My name, I will do it." (John 14:13 NKJV). Don't just think more, think big. Think out of the box. Many times in life, the answer to the issue or the problem is thinking outside of the box of our circumstances.

Nelson Mandela said, "There is no passion to be found playing small, settling for a life that is less than the one you are capable of."

If you do what you have always done, you will get what you have always got. The answer isn't in the ordinary. It's going to take bigger thinking to take you forward. You need to play differently to get a new positive result. That's when the passion arrives – and when you have the passion, you have the strength and the inspiration to play at a higher level.

freedomcentre
the church on the docks

The freedomcentre is a church and a vision for all sorts of people from different journeys, experiences and locations. All of us are here to show the city of Preston that all things are possible to those who believe! We believe in FREEDOM because that's what God has promised.

We meet every Sunday from 10.30am

www.thefreedomcentre.com
contact@thefreedomcentre.com

Unit 6, Hardy Close, Ashton, Preston PR2 2XP

Jack & Susan McVicar
Pastors and Founders

jackbmcvicar.com

Charity Reg 1106874

Luv Preston is a charity Sue and I founded shortly after beginning the freedomcentre in order to serve the disadvantaged in our city. We serve over 5,000 meals per year in our drop-in and Foodbank.

10% OF ALL BOOK SALES GOES TOWARDS **LUV PRESTON**

Charity Reg 1129452